Anonymous

A Psalmody for the New Church

Containing the First Fifty Psalms and Other Selections from the Word

Anonymous

A Psalmody for the New Church
Containing the First Fifty Psalms and Other Selections from the Word

ISBN/EAN: 9783744778961

Printed in Europe, USA, Canada, Australia, Japan

Cover: Foto ©Lupo / pixelio.de

More available books at **www.hansebooks.com**

A Psalmody

for

The New Church

Containing

The first fifty Psalms and other Selections
from the Word

Published by
The Academy of the New Church
Philadelphia

COPYRIGHT, 1898, BY THE ACADEMY OF THE NEW CHURCH.

PREFACE.

This work is offered to the kindly consideration of the members of the New Church.

It is written *for the New Church*, being based upon a recognition of the fact that, in the Word of God, there is an internal or spiritual sense, in the understanding of which the Church is to be; and, as it is believed that this is probably the first published musical work of the kind, some indulgence is craved for those who, so far, enter upon untrodden ground.

The short statements of the "internal sense" of the Psalms, are taken from the work of Emanuel Swedenborg, entitled "A Summary Exposition of the Internal Sense of the Prophets and Psalms," and may be read aloud where placed.

A new translation of the original hebrew text of the Psalms has been made; and the selections from other parts of the Word, which are appended, have also been re-translated, and a summary of their spiritual sense extracted from the Writings of Swedenborg.

The translation is by the Rev. E. S. Price, A. B., Th. B., and others, and the music by Mr. C. J. Whittington.

A feature of the musical treatment is, that there is no repetition of the words, and that antiphony is frequently made use of.

The vocal parts and accompaniments, being printed in the condensed form known as "short score," involve occasional obscurities; but the issue of the work in any other form must have added greatly to its bulk and cost.

The accompaniments, as written, will be found practicable upon an organ having pedals, and also upon the pianoforte; but some management will be required, here and there, to render the accompaniment upon the latter instrument; and in some cases the use of four hands is necessary. But the idea of an orchestral accompaniment has been kept in view; for, as we read, "The *sounds* of musical instruments elevate the affection, and the *truths* form it;" and, "The Psalms of David are called 'Psalms' from playing on stringed instruments, and also 'Songs' from singing; for they were played and sung together with the adjoined sounds of various instruments" (A. E. 323); and further, "As instruments of every kind, from correspondence, signified the delightful and pleasant things of spiritual and celestial affections, on many of the Psalms there is an inscription indicating how they were to be played; as 'upon Neginoth,' 'upon Nehiloth,' 'upon the Octave,' etc. (A. C. 8337)." "Let no one believe that so many instruments would have been mentioned unless each signified something" (A. C. 420).

Praise Him with the sound of the trumpet,
Praise Him with psalter and harp.
Praise Him with timbrel and dance,
Praise Him with stringed instruments and organ.
Praise Him with cymbals of hearing,
Praise Him with cymbals of shouting.
Let every soul praise the Lord!
  Praise ye the Lord.

CONTENTS.

THE FIRST FIFTY PSALMS.

	PAGE
PSALM I,	1
" II,	3
" III,	8
" IV,	10
" V,	12
" VI,	16
" VII,	18
" VIII,	23
" IX,	26
" X,	34
" XI,	39
" XII,	41
" XIII,	43
" XIV,	45
" XV,	48
" XVI,	51
" XVII,	54
" XVIII,	58
" XIX,	82
" XX,	87
" XXI,	89
" XXII,	93
" XXIII,	105
" XXIV,	107
" XXV,	113
" XXVI,	123
" XXVII,	126
" XXVIII,	131
" XXIX,	135
" XXX,	140
" XXXI,	144
" XXXII,	154
" XXXIII,	160
" XXXIV,	169
" XXXV,	181
" XXXVI,	193
" XXXVII,	197
" XXXVIII,	229
" XXXIX,	240
" XL,	247
" XLI,	259
" XLII,	267
" XLIII,	276
" XLIV,	283
" XLV,	298
" XLVI,	316
" XLVII,	321
" XLVIII,	325
" XLIX,	330
" L,	341

OTHER SELECTIONS FROM THE WORD.

	PAGE
DEUTERONOMY VI·4, 5. Shema Yisrael (Heb.),	382
NUMBERS XXIV.5, 6. How good are thy tents,	353
PSALM V·8. I come into Thy house,	350
" LI·19. The sacrifices of God,	355
" XCIII.5. Thy testimonies are very sure,	358
" CXVI 12-14. What shall I render?..	361
" CXXII·6, 7. Pray for the peace of Jerusalem,	356
" CXXXII:8, 9, 13, 14. Arise, O LORD,	358
" CL, (Hebrew),	382
ISAIAH VI:3. Holy, holy, holy,	359
" XII:2, 3. Behold, the God of my salvation,	362
" XXX:26. And the light of the moon,	363
" XL:3-5. The voice of one,	360
JEREMIAH XVII:7, 8. Blessed the man,	364
HABAKKUK II:20. The LORD is in the temple of His holiness,	362
MATTHEW VII.7, 8. Ask, and it shall be given,	365
" XI·28-30. Come unto Me,	370
" XIX·14. Suffer the infants and forbid them not,	379
" XXI:9. Hosanna,	366
LUKE II:14. Doxa en hupsistois, (Greek)	381
JOHN III:8. The wind doth breathe where it willeth,	359
" III:16. For God so loved the world,	363
" IV:13-15. Whosoever drinketh,	368
" IV:23, 24. The hour cometh and now is,	369
" V:39. Search the Scriptures,	371
" XI:25, 26. I am the Resurrection,	372
APOCALYPSE I:4-8. Grace be unto you,	373
" I·17, 18. Fear not,	376
" II:7. To him that overcometh,	376
" III:20. Behold, I stand at the door, and knock,	377
" III:22. He that hath an ear,	365
" IV:8. Hagios, Hagios, Hagios (Gr.),	387
" V·13. To Him that sitteth upon the throne,	377
" XI·16-18. We give thanks unto Thee,	378
" XIV:7. Fear ye God,	379
" XIV:13. Happy are the dead who die in the LORD,	372
" XV 3, 4. Great and wonderful are Thy works,	380
" XIX.1, 2 Alleluia,	375
" XX·6. Happy and holy,	371

PSALM I.

The New Church in place of the Former. The Church totally devastated, and its Rejection. The Last Judgment by the Lord.

The man who doth not live ill, is regenerated by the Word of the Lord.

PSALM II.

The successive Vastation of the Church. The Church totally devastated, and its Rejection. The Lord's Advent, and the New Church in place of the Former. The Glorification of the Human of the Lord, or Unition with the Divine.

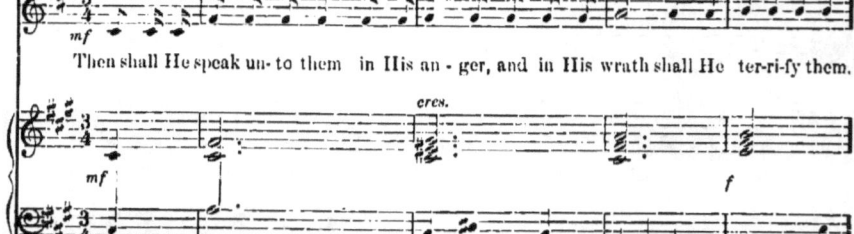

And He will disperse the falses of evil.

Let them therefore acknowledge and worship the Divine Human of the Lord, lest they perish.

PSALM III.

The Temptations of the Lord in general. The State of Humiliation before the Father.

Concerning the Lord, when He was in temptations and subjugated the hells, and then in a state of humiliation, in which He prayed to the Father.

A Psalm of David; when he fled from Absalom his son.

Andante moderato ♩ = 96.

O Lord, how are mul - ti - plied mine en - - e - mies;........
Voices in unison.

ma - - ny are ris - ing up a - gainst...... me.........

Ma - ny are say - ing of my soul, There is no sal-vation for him in God.
cres. *dim.* *rall.*

Se - lah. But Thou, O Lord, art a shield for me; my glo - ry, and the up-
Harmony. Unison.
pp *cres.*

lift - er of my head. With my voice un - to the Lord I cry, and He an - swer-eth
p
cres.

me from the mount - ain of His ho - - li - - ness.
dim. *rall.*

PSALM III. *Concluded.* 9

PSALM IV.

The Temptations of the Lord even to Despair.   The Lord's Advent.

Concerning the Lord, when in great temptations.

Of the Conqueror; upon Neginoth; a Psalm; of David.

When I cry, an-swer me, O God of my jus-tice, in anguish give breadth to me; be gra-cious un-to me, and hear my pray'r. Ye sons of man, how long will my glo-ry be for shame, will ye love van-i-ty, will ye seek a lie?... Se- lah.

They should fear Him, because from the Father He hath protection.

And know ye, that the Lord mak-eth won-der-ful the Ho-ly One for Him-self; the Lord hear-eth when I cry...... un-to Him.

Exhortation to repent.

PSALM V.

The State of the Lord's Humiliation before the Father. His Combats with the Hells.

Prayer of the Lord to the Father, that He would assist.

Of the Conqueror, upon Nechiloth, a Psalm of David.

Moderato ♩=92.

To my say-ings give ear, O Lord, un-der-stand my med-i-ta-tion. Heark-en to the voice of my cry, my King, and my God; for un-to to the Thee I pray. O Lord, in the morn-ing Thou wilt hear my voice; in the morn-ing I will dis-pose my-self un-to Thee, and will watch.

Against the evil, falsifiers and hypocrites.

f Unison.

For not a God de-light-ing in wick-ed-ness art Thou, e-vil a-

Prayer of the Lord to the Father, that He would assist.

14   PSALM V. *Continued.*

in Thy fear. O Lord, lead me in Thy jus-tice, be-cause of mine op-pres-sors; make straight be-fore my face Thy way.

Against the evil, falsifiers and hypocrites.

mf Unison.

For noth-ing in the mouth of an-y-one is right, their bel-ly is per-di-tion, an o-pen sep-ul-chre their throat; with their tongue they flat-ter. Make them guil-ty, O God, let them fall by their own coun-sels; by

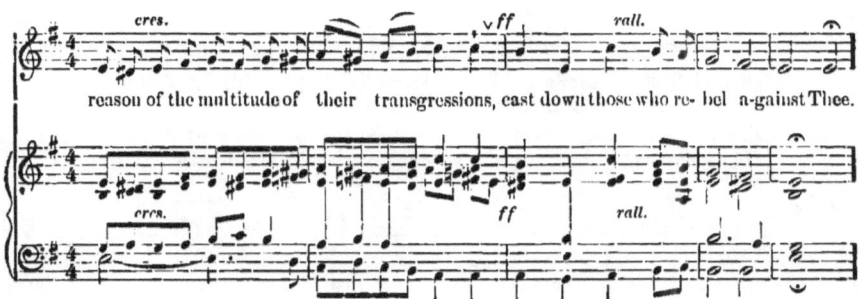

Prayer of the Lord to the Father, that He would assist.

PSALM VI.

The State of the Lord's Humiliation before the Father. His Temptations even to Despair. His Victory over the Hells.

Prayer of the Lord to the Father, when He was in the last state of temptations, which state is despair.

Of the Conqueror; on Neginoth; upon the Sheminith; a Psalm; of David.

Larghetto. ♩ = 63.

O Lord, do not in Thine an-ger re-buke me, nor in Thy wrath chastise me. Have mer-cy up-on me, O Lord, for lan-guish-ing am I; heal me, O Lord, for dis-turb-ed are my bones. And my soul is disturb-ed might-i-ly; and Thou, O Lord, how long? Re-

poco accell. ♩ = 88. *rall.* *a tempo 1mo.*

turn, O Lord, res-cue my soul; save me, for the sake of Thy mer - cy. For there is not in death, re-membrance of Thee; in hell, who shall con-fess Thee? I am wea-ry with my sigh-ing, thro' the whole night I wash my bed; with my tears my couch I

PSALM VI. *Concluded.*

drench. Mine eye wasteth away from in-dig-na - tion, it waxeth old among all mine en - e-mies.

And being assisted, He repressed the hells.

Allegro moderato. ♩ = 126.

De-part from me, all ye workers of in - i - qui-ty, for the LORD hath heard the voice of my weep - ing. The LORD hath heard my sup - pli - ca - tion; the LORD........ will re - ceive my prayer. Asham-ed and dis-turb - ed might - i - ly are all.............. mine en - e - mies; they turn........ back, they are a - sham - - ed sud - den - ly.

cres.

Unison.

Harmony.

rall.

PSALM VII.

The State of the Lord's Humiliation before the Father. His Combats with the Hells. His Victory over them.

Prayer of the Lord to the Father, that He assist against the hells.

Shiggaion, of David, which he sang to the LORD, upon the words of Kush, the Benjamite.

O LORD my God, in Thee do I confide; save me from all my persecutors, and rescue me. Lest they seize as a lion my soul,......... rending, but none......... rescuing.

Because He is just and hath no evil.

O LORD my God, if I have done this, if there be perversity in my hands. If I have rendered evil to him that is at peace with me, and have despoiled mine enemy without cause.

PSALM VII. *Continued.*

Prayer of the Lord to the Father, that He assist against the hells, because He is just, and hath no evil.

PSALM VII. *Continued.*

Prayer of the Lord to the Father, that He assist against the hells.

PSALM VII. *Concluded.*

PSALM VIII.

The State of the Lord's Humiliation before the Father. His Combats with the Hells. The Glorification of His Human, or Unition with the Divine.

Celebration of the Father by the Lord, that He regard His innocence and assist against the hells.

Of the Conqueror; upon Gittith; a Psalm; of David.

PSALM IX.

Celebration and Worship of the Lord. The State of His Humiliation before the Father. His Victory over the Hells, or the Subjugation of them.

Thanksgiving and joy of the Lord because the evil have been judged and destroyed.

Of the Conquerer, upon Muth-labben, a Psalm of David.

Thanksgiving and joy of the Lord because the evil have been judged and destroyed.

PSALM X.

The Church totally devastated and its Rejection. The Last Judgment by the Lord.

The evil do evil to the good, and deny God, and are hypocrites and deceivers.

Molto Moderato ♩ = 66.

I and II. Wherefore, O LORD, standest Thou a-far off; hid-est Thyself in times of an-guish? In the pride of the wick-ed he per-se-cut-eth the af-flict-ed; they are caught in the de-vic-es which they have thought out. For the wick-ed glor-i-eth ov-er the lust of his soul, and the cov-et-ous he bless-eth, he de-spis-eth the LORD. The wick-ed, ac-cord-ing to the lift-ing up of his nos-tril, seek-eth nothing; there is no God, are all his thoughts. Tort-uous are his ways at all times, on high are Thy judg-ments be-fore

PSALM XI.

The Combats of the Lord with the Hells. Victory over them, or Subjugation of them.

The Lord exciteth Himself to fight against the evil for the good.

Of the Conqueror; of David.

Moderato ♩ = 88.

In the Lord do I con-fide; how say ye to my soul, Flee in-to your mountain as a bird? For be-hold, the wick-ed bend the bow, they pre-pare their ar-row up-on the string, to shoot in darkness the upright in heart. For the foun-da-tions are o-ver-turned; the just, what shall he do? The Lord is in the tem-ple of His ho-li-ness; the Lord, in heav-en is His throne; His eyes see, His eye-lids prove the

PSALM XIII.

Temptations of the Lord even to despair. Victory over the Hells, or their Subjugation.

Concerning the state of the temptations of the Lord, and concerning the grievous insurrection of the infernals against Him.

Of the Conqueror; a Psalm of David.

PSALM XIV.

The Church totally devastated and its Rejection. The Rejection of the Lord by the Church. Redemption and Salvation from the Lord.

There is no longer any understanding of truth nor will of good.

Of the Conqueror; of David.

They are against good and truth.

The Lord will save those who are of the Church, whence they will have joy from Him.

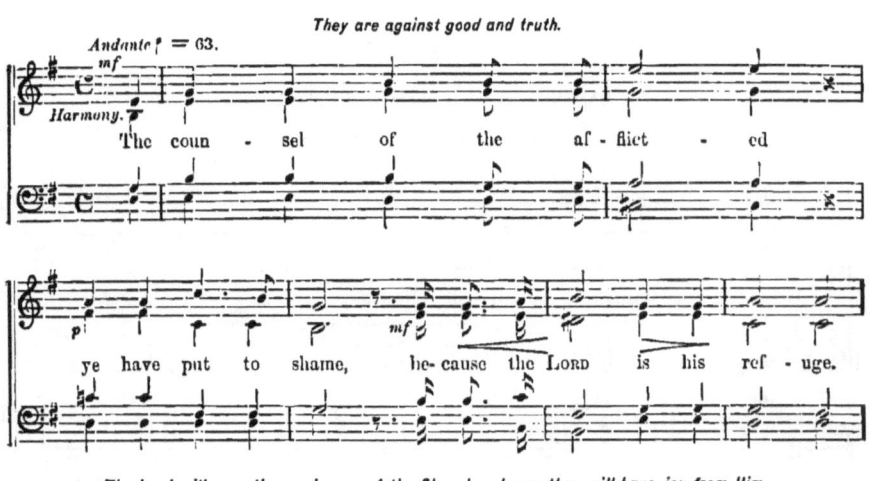

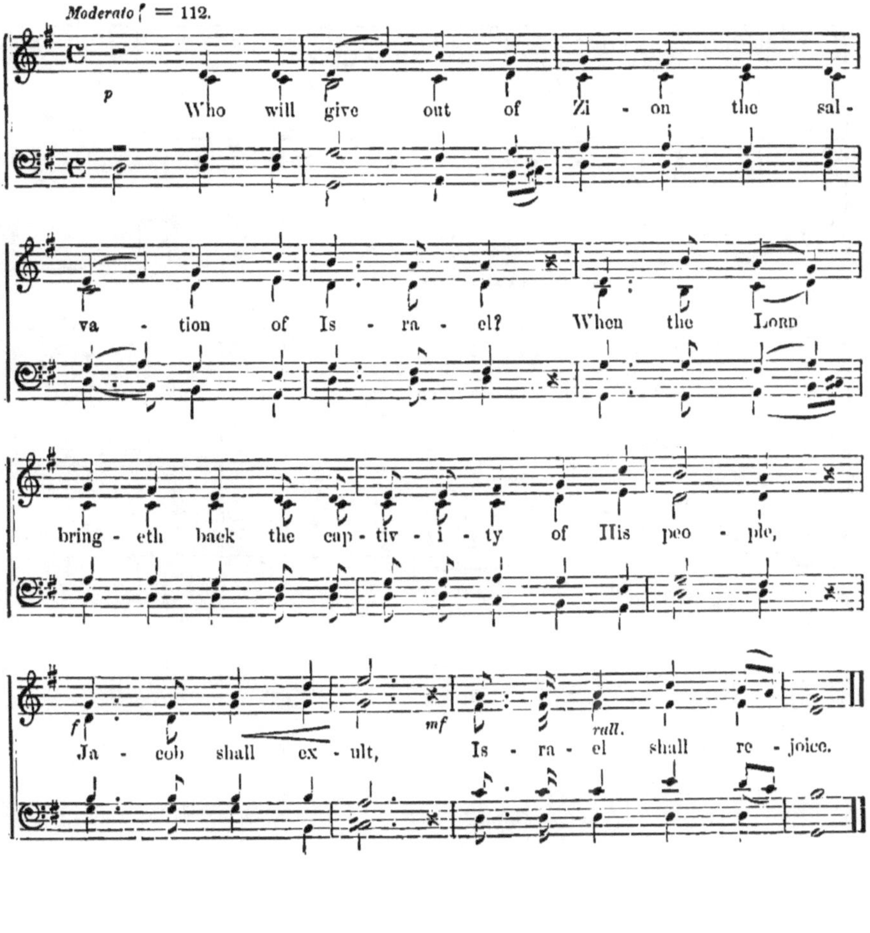

PSALM XV.

The New Church in place of the Former.

They who love the neighbor and God, will be of the Church of the Lord.

A Psalm of David.

PSALM XV. *Continued.* 49

From the Divine within Himself.

From which He is sustained against the evil, who rise up against Him.

PSALM XVIII.

The Combats of the Lord with the Hells, and His Victory over them, or the Subjugation of them. The New Church in place of the Former. Celebration and Worship of the Lord, and Redemption and Salvation by Him.

Combats of the Lord with the hells.

Trust of the Lord from His Divine, against the hells with which He fought.

The Lord had justice and integrity.

The Lord also had Divine Truth.

PSALM XVIII. Continued.

The Lord had justice and integrity.

He is the only God.

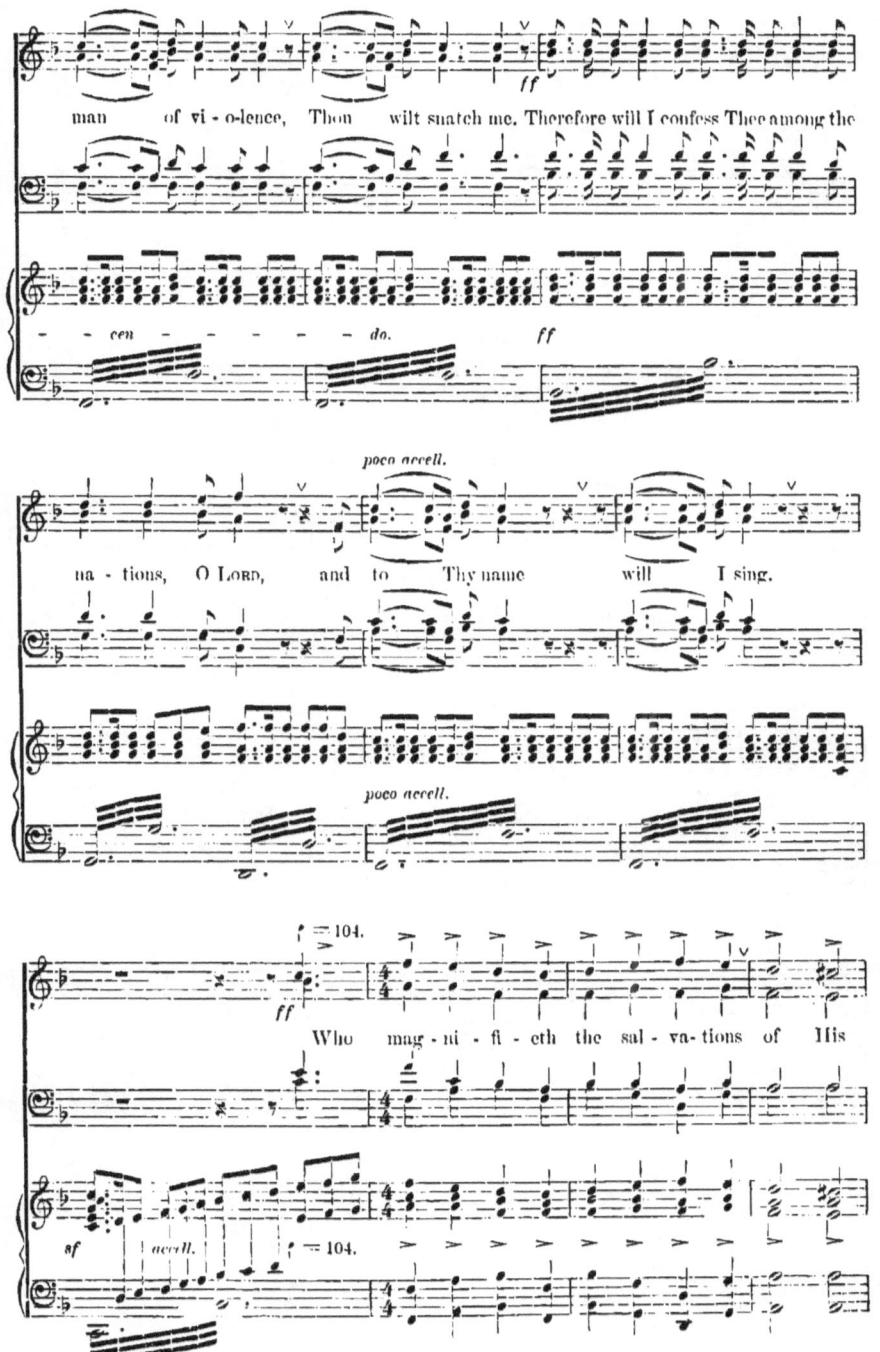

PSALM XIX.

The New Church in place of the Former. The New Church, and at the same time the New Heaven.

The Divine Truth will go forth on every side.

Of the Conqueror; a Psalm; of David.

PSALM XIX. *Continued.*

speech and no word, where their voice is not heard. In-to all............ the earth hath gone forth their line, and un-to the end of the world, their word; for the sun he hath set......... a tent....... in them.

This is from the Lord, from the firsts to the ultimates of heaven and the church.

And he as a bride-groom go-ing forth from his cham-ber, he re-joi-ceth as a he-ro to run a course. From the end of the heav-ens is his go-ing forth, and his cir-cuit un-to the

The Divine Truth perfecteth man, because it is wisdom.

PSALM XX.

Celebration and Worship of the Lord. Redemption and Salvation by Him. The Church totally devastated and its Rejection.

Celebration of the Lord that He sustains the church.

Of the Conqueror; a Psalm; of David.

PSALM XXI.

The Glorification of the Human of the Lord, or Unition with the Divine. His Victory over the Hells, or their Subjugation, and the Last Judgment by Him.

Concerning the Lord: From His Divine He hath all good and truth, thus honor and glory.

Of the Conqueror; a Psalm; of David.

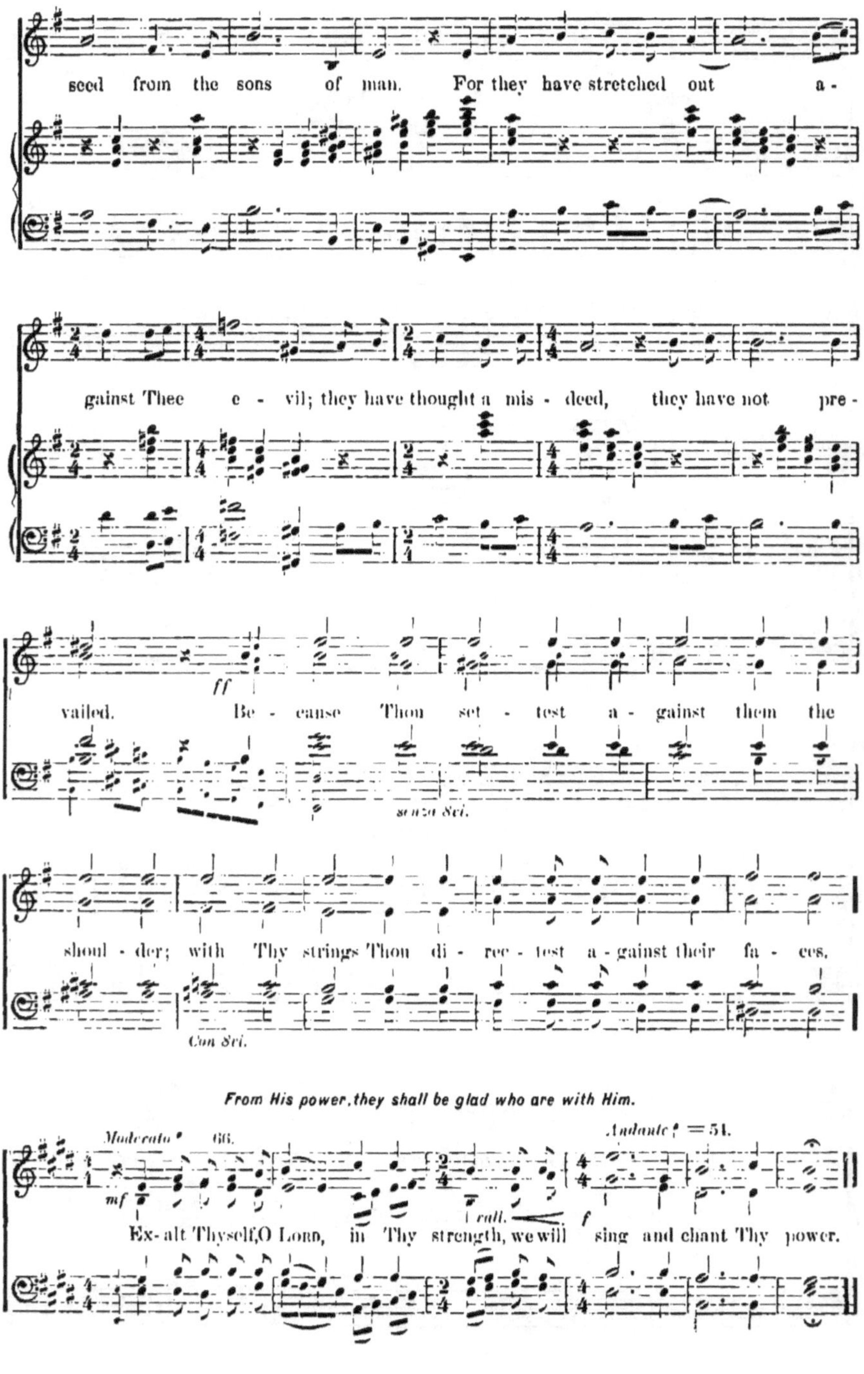
seed from the sons of man. For they have stretched out a -
gainst Thee e - vil; they have thought a mis - deed, they have not pre -
vailed. Be - cause Thou set - test a - gainst them the
ff
senza Sci.
shoul - der; with Thy strings Thou di - rec - test a - gainst their fa - ces.
Con Sci.
From His power, they shall be glad who are with Him.
Moderato ♩ 66.
Andante ♩ = 54.
mf
rall.
f
Ex - alt Thyself, O Lord, in Thy strength, we will sing and chant Thy power.

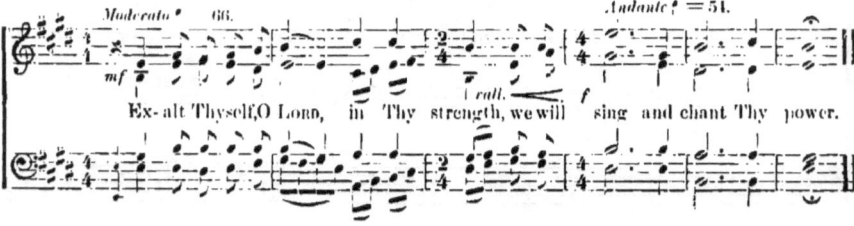

PSALM XXII.

The Passion of the Cross. The Rejection of the Lord by the Church. The Temptations of the Lord even to Despair. The New Church in place of the Former.

The state of the Passion of the Lord. Prayer to the Father that He be not forsaken.
Of the Conqueror; upon the Hind of the Dawn; a Psalm; of David.

From conception He is of Himself.

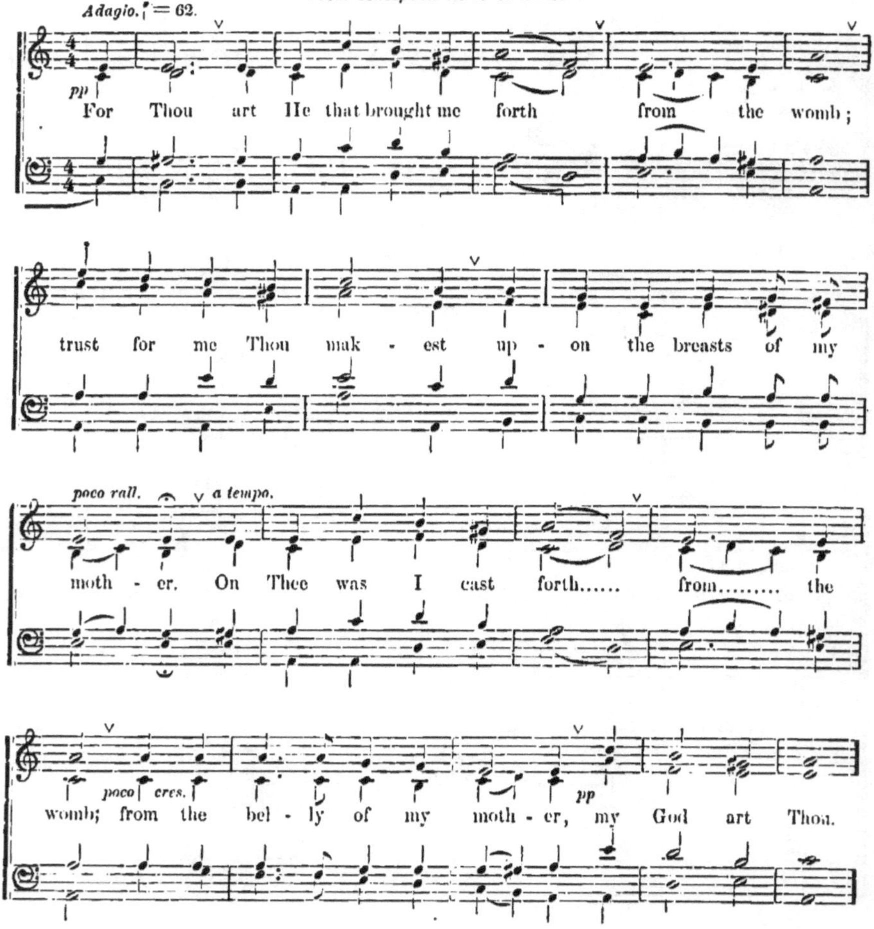

They who are of the church where the Word is, have condemmed Him to death.

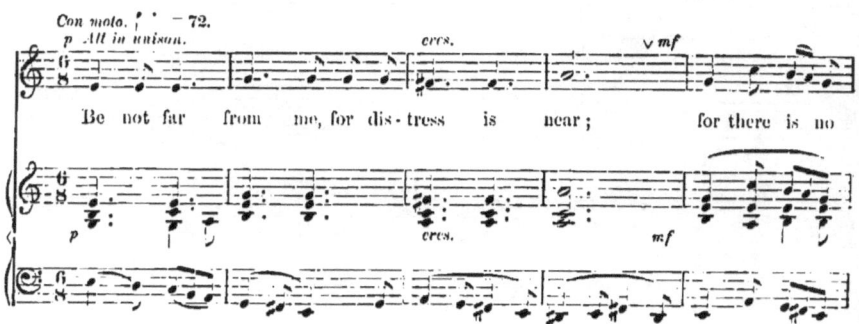

PSALM XXII. Continued.

They have crucified Him.

They have dissipated the truths of His Word.

PSALM XXII. Continued.

PSALM XXIV.

The New Church in place of the Former. Redemption and Salvation by the Lord.

Concerning the church, which is from the Lord by the Word.

Of David; a Psalm.

PSALM XXV.

Celebration and Worship of the Lord. The New Church in place of the Former. Redemption and Salvation by the Lord. His Combats with the Hells.

Prayer of the church to the Lord, that they may be guarded from the hells.

Of David.

That they may be taught in truths.

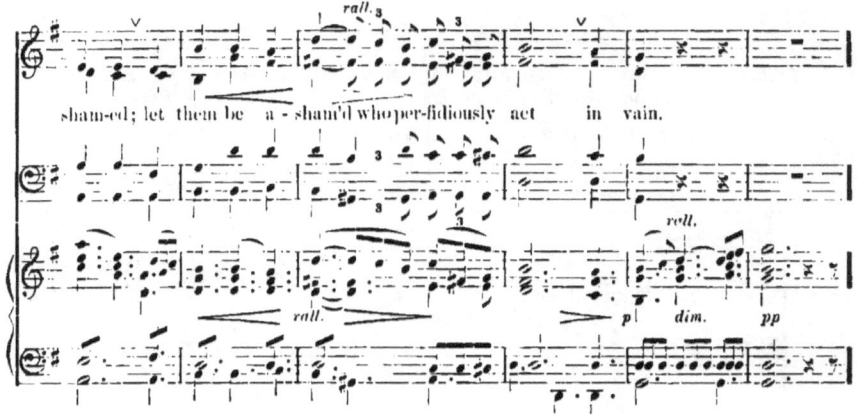

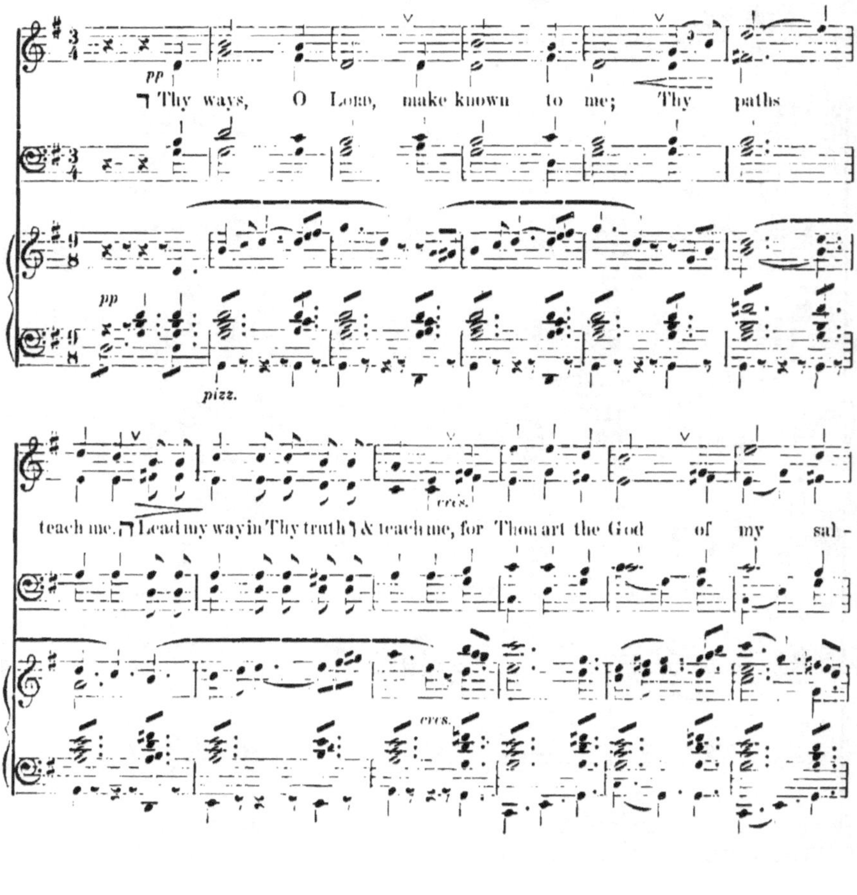

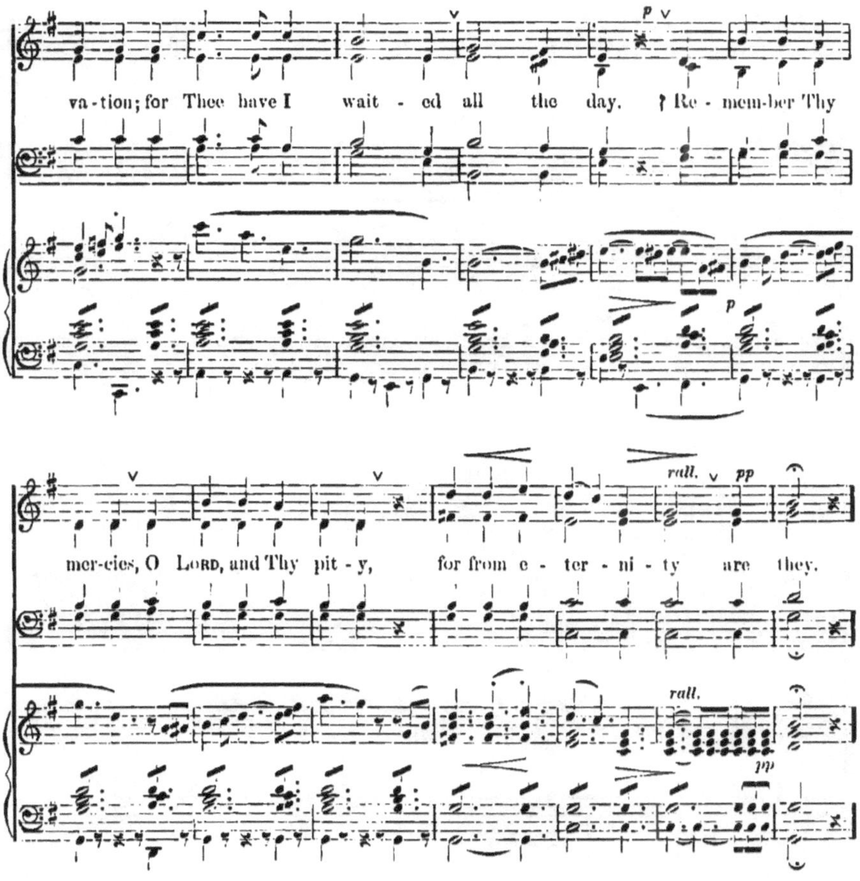

That their sins may be remitted, from mercy.

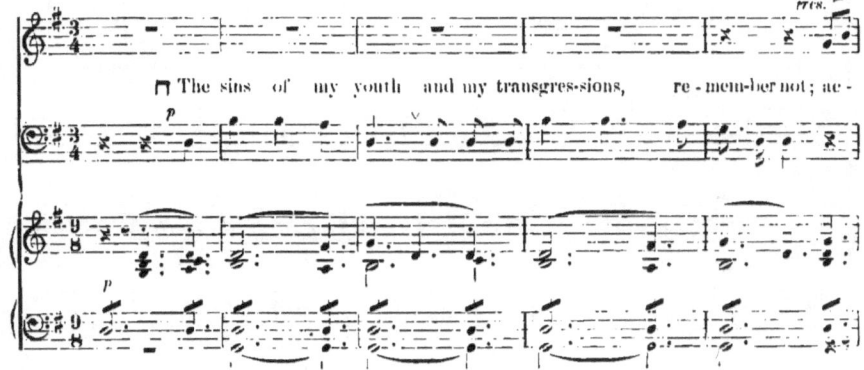

Thus they have good and conjunction.

Prayer of the church to the Lord, and in the supreme sense, of the Lord to the Father, that because He alone combats, He would assist against the hells.

PSALM XXVI.

Celebration and Worship of the Lord, His Combats with the Hells, and Redemption and Salvation by Him.

Con expressione. ♩ = 52.
mf
con 8vi.
pp
mf
p
con 8vi.
cres.
rall.
mf
p
pp

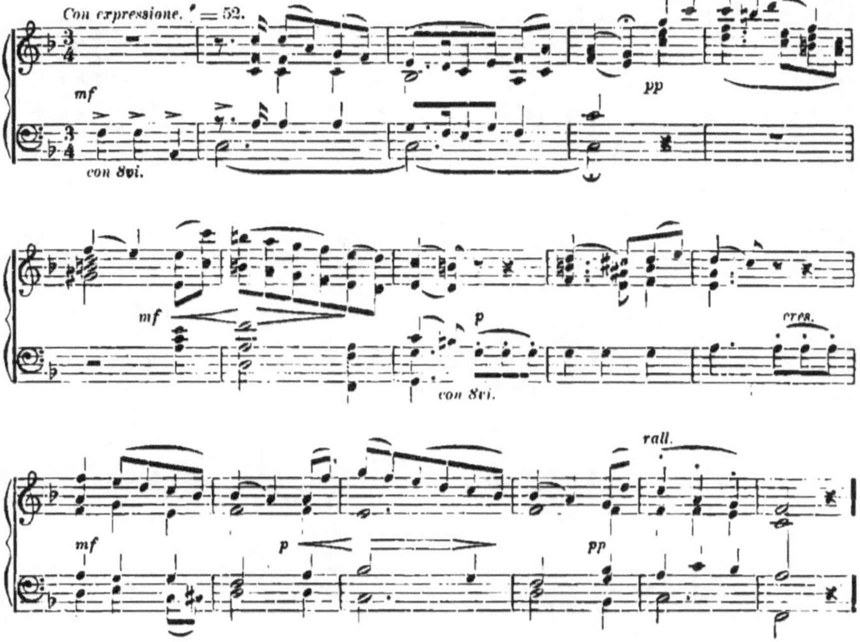

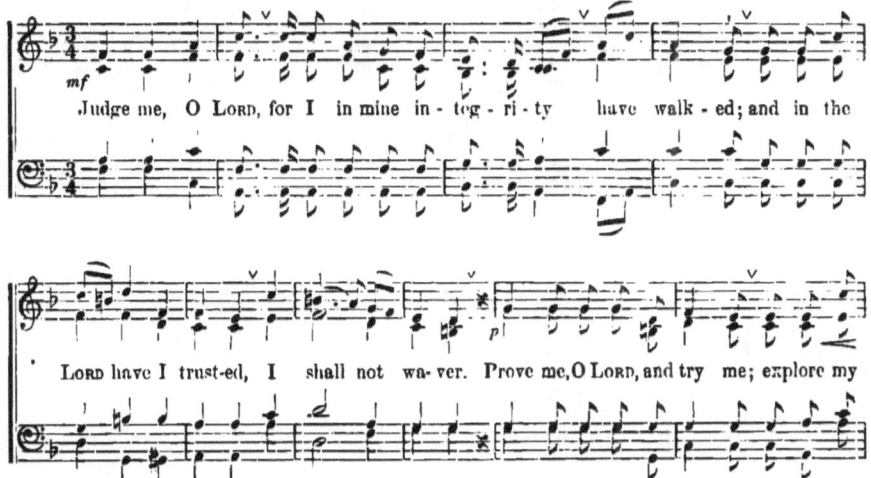

The Lord has integrity, purity, and innocence.

Of David.

mf
Judge me, O Lord, for I in mine in - teg - ri - ty have walk - ed; and in the
Lord have I trust-ed, I shall not wa- ver. Prove me, O Lord, and try me; explore my
p

PSALM XXVII.

The Combats of the Lord with the Hells. His Victory over them, or the Subjugation of them, and the Glorification of His Human, or Unition with the Divine.

Discourse of the Lord with the Father, that He does not fear the hells which fight against Him.

Of David.

128   PSALM XXVII. *Continued.*

131

PSALM XXVIII.

The State of the Lord's Humiliation before the Father, and His Victory over the Hells, or the Subjugation of them. Redemption and Salvation by the Lord.

Prayer of the Lord to the Father, that the hypocrites may be subjugated,

Of David.

Un-to Thee, O Lord, I cry; my Rock, be not

PSALM XXVIII. Concluded.

The Father assists, and He will prevail.

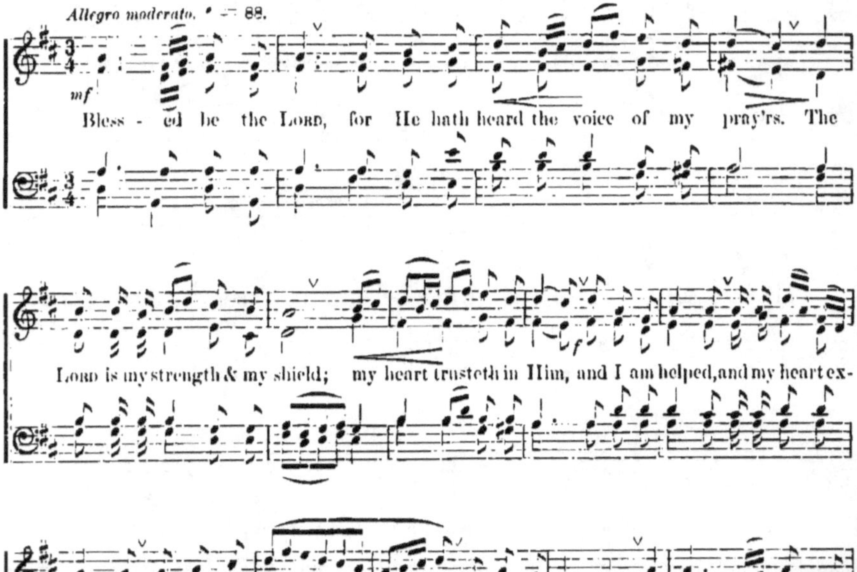

Allegro moderato. ♩ = 88.

Bless - ed be the Lord, for He hath heard the voice of my pray'rs. The Lord is my strength & my shield; my heart trusteth in Him, and I am helped, and my heart ex- ult - eth, and with my song.......... I will confess Him. The Lord is strength for them, and the sav - ing strength of His a - noint - ed, is He.

poco rall.

Prayer that they may be saved, who are in the truths and goods of the church.

Adagio.
Unison.   *Harmony.*   *Unison.*
pp   *pp*

Save Thy peo-ple, & bless Thine in-heritance; and feed them, & up- lift them, to e- ter - ni- ty.

PSALM XXIX.

The Glorification of the Human of the Lord, or Unition with the Divine, and the New Church in place of the Former.

Allegro maestoso. ♩ = 63.
p
f
pp
pp

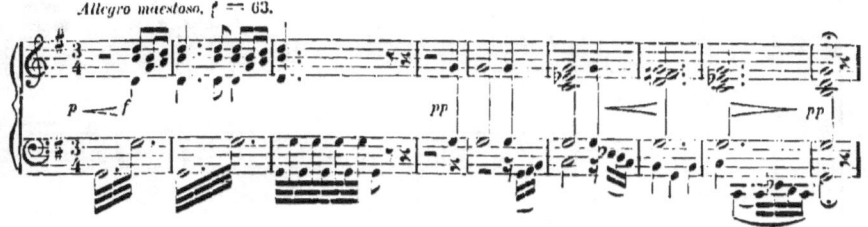

They who are in truths from the Word, will adore the Lord, Who is the Word.

A Psalm; of David.

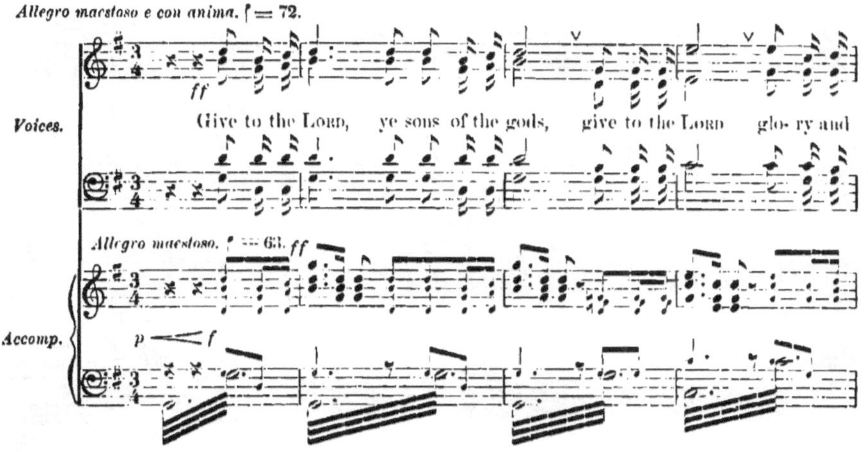
Allegro maestoso e con anima. ♩ = 72.
ff
Voices.
Give to the Lord, ye sons of the gods, give to the Lord glo- ry and
Allegro maestoso. ♩ = 63.
ff
Accomp.
p
f

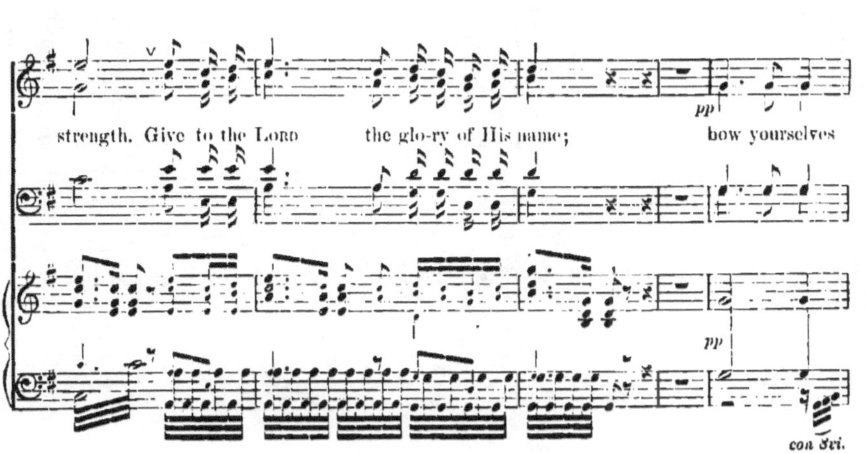
strength. Give to the Lord the glo-ry of His name; bow yourselves
pp
pp
con 8vi.

PSALM XXIX. *Continued.*

The Power of Divine Truth from the Lord.

PSALM XXX.

The Glorification of the Human of the Lord, or Unition with the Divine, and the Passion of the Cross.

The Glorification of the Human of the Lord after He had suffered temptations, and the last, which was that of the Cross.

A Psalm; a Song of the Dedication of the House; of David.

I will ex-alt Thee, O Lord, for Thou hast up-lift-ed me, nor

PSALM XXXI.

The State of the Lord's Humiliation before the Father, and His Combats with the Hells. The Passion of the Cross, and the Rejection of the Lord by the Church. The Temptations of the Lord even to Despair.

Prayer of the Lord to the Father, that He protect against those who devise evil.
Of the Conqueror; a Psalm; of David.

In Thee, O Lord, have I trust-ed, let me not be a-sham-ed to e-ter-ni-ty; in Thy jus-tice de-liv-er me. In-cline un-to me Thine ear,

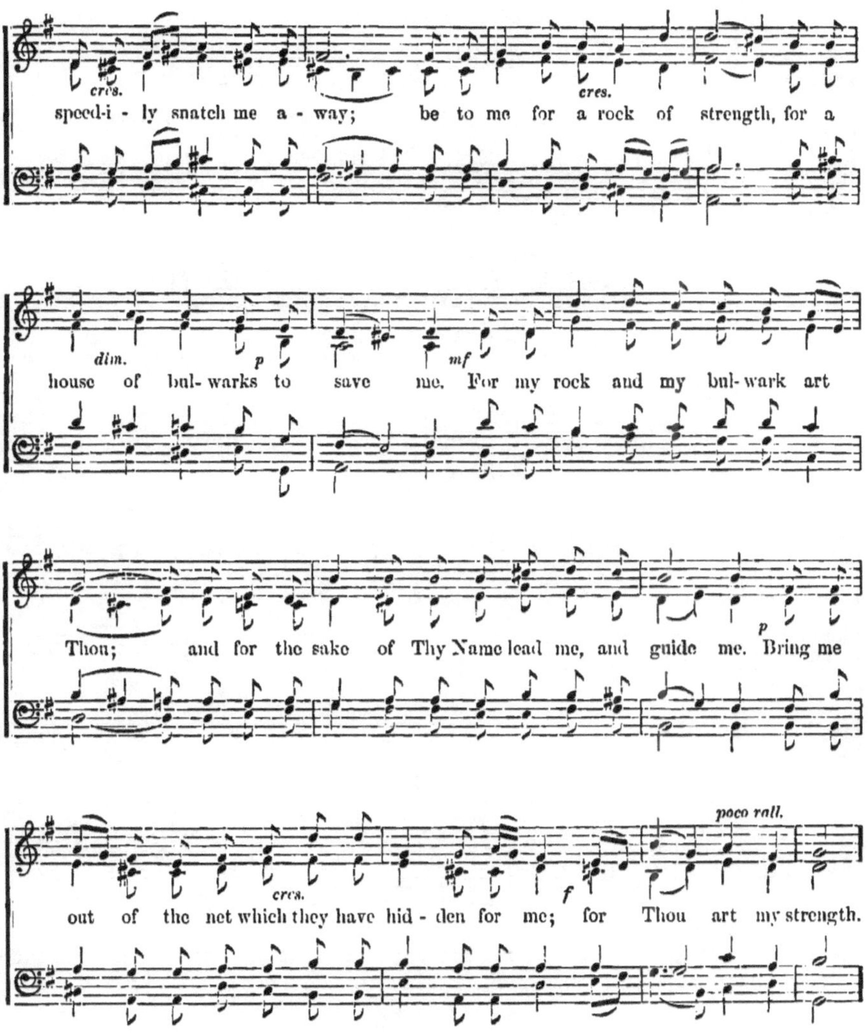
cres.
cres.
speed-i - ly snatch me a - way; be to me for a rock of strength, for a
dim.
p
mf
house of bul- warks to save me. For my rock and my bul- wark art
p
Thou; and for the sake of Thy Name lead me, and guide me. Bring me
poco rall.
cres.
f
out of the net which they have hid - den for me; for Thou art my strength.

And who wish to kill Him.

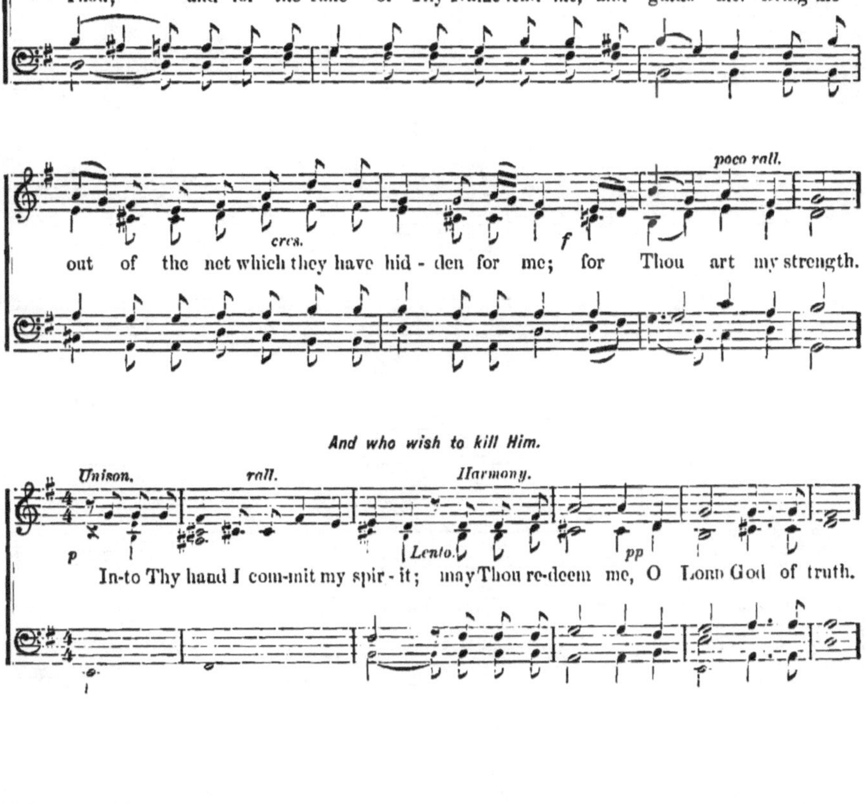
Unison.
rall.
Harmony.
p
Lento.
pp
In-to Thy hand I com-mit my spir - it; may Thou re-deem me, O Lord God of truth.

Whence He has grief of heart.

PSALM XXXII.

The Temptations of the Lord even to Despair.

The just one is happy.
Of David; making intelligent.

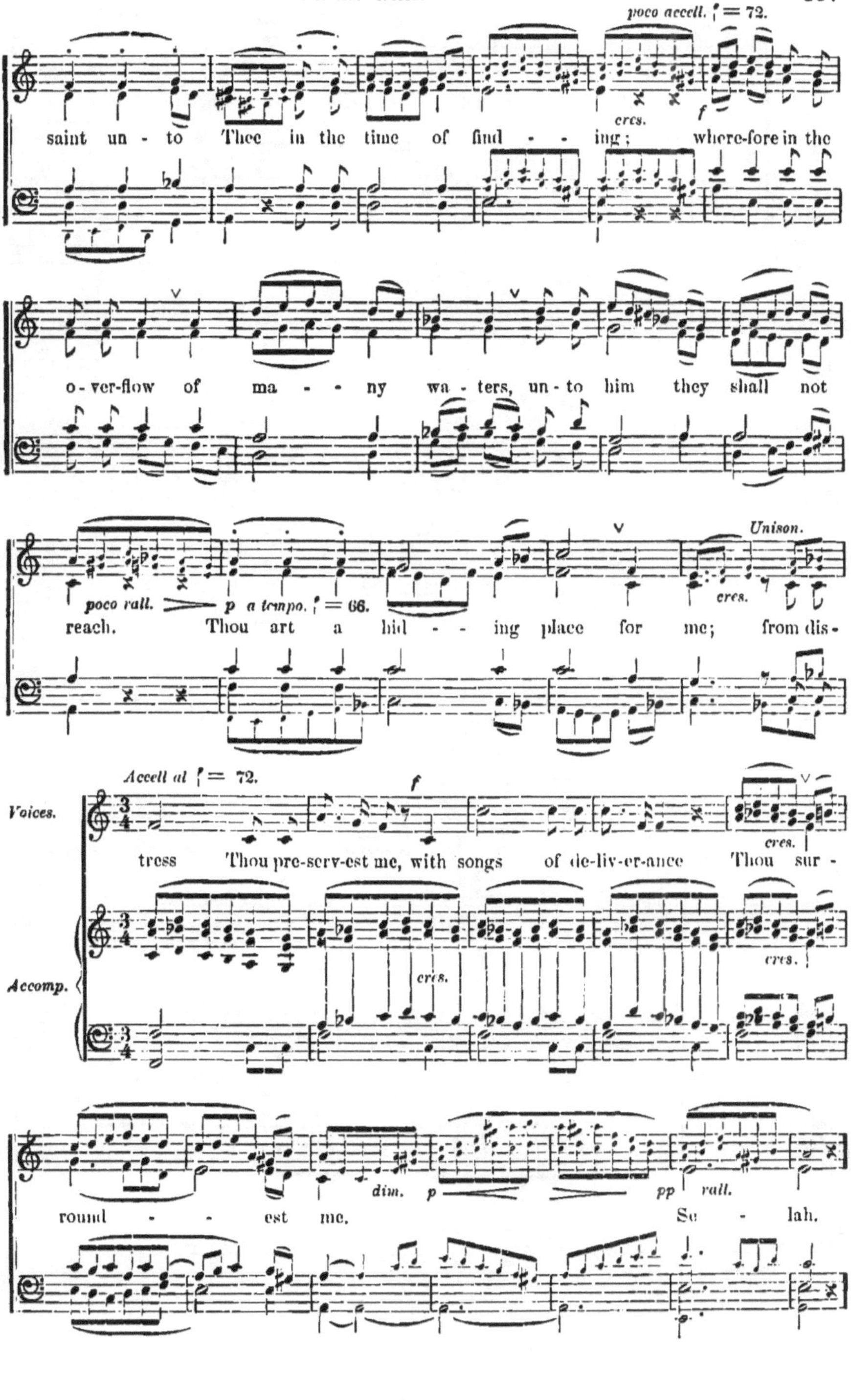
poco accell. = 72.
cres.
f
saint un - to Thee in the time of find - - ing; where-fore in the
o - ver-flow of ma - - ny wa - ters, un - to him they shall not
poco rall.
p a tempo. = 66.
Unison.
cres.
reach. Thou art a hid - - ing place for me; from dis -
Accell al = 72.
Voices.
f
tress Thou pre-serv-est me, with songs of de-liv-er-ance Thou sur -
cres.
Accomp.
cres.
cres.
dim. p
pp rall.
round - - est me. Se - lah.

PSALM XXXIII.

Celebration and Worship of the Lord. The Church totally devasted, and its Rejection. The New Church in place of the Former. Redemption and Salvation by the Lord.

Celebration of the Lord because from Him is the church, by the Word.

Sing, ye just, in the Lord; for the up-right, come-ly is

162 PSALM XXXIII. *Continued.*

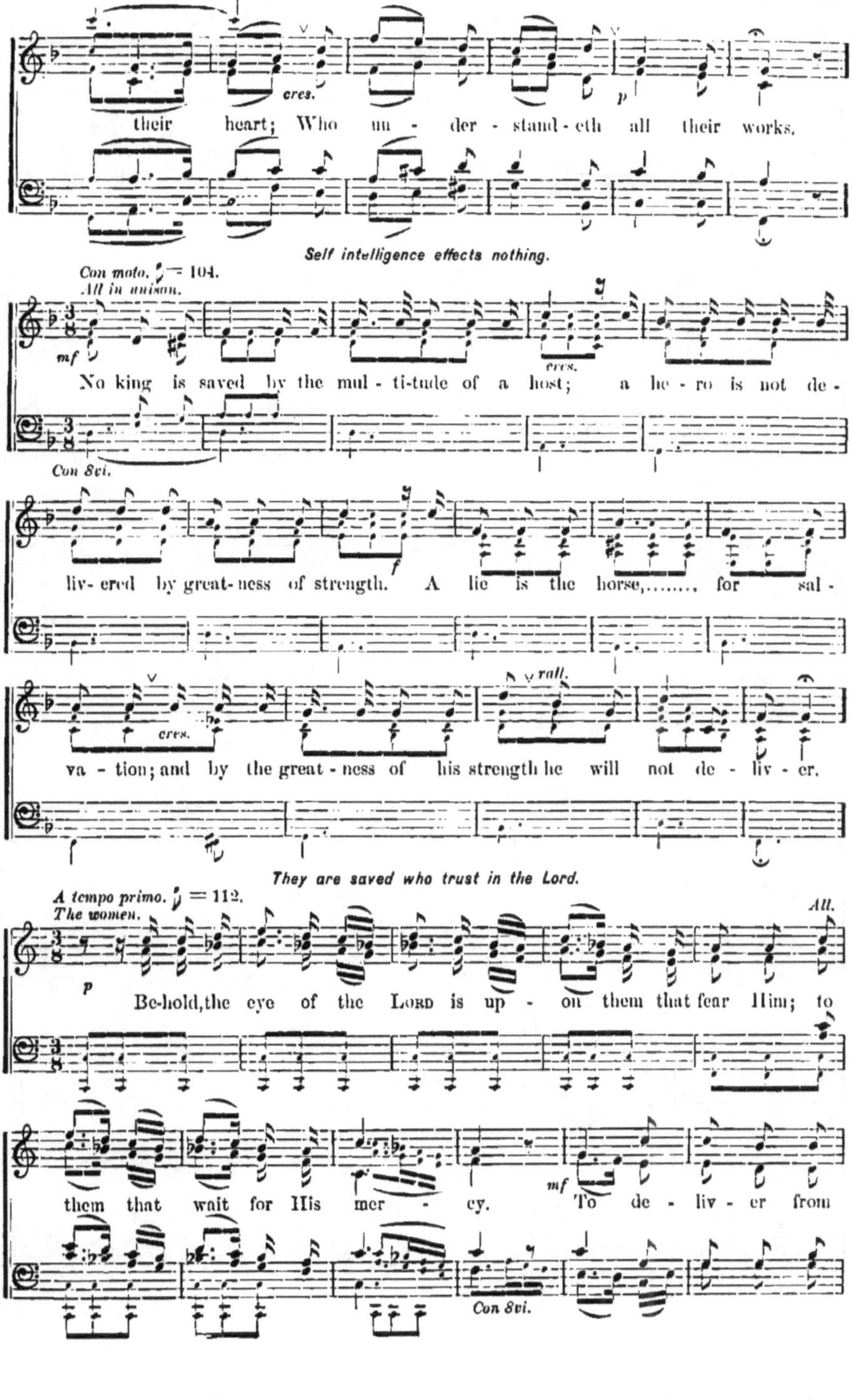
cres.
p
their heart; Who un - der - stand - eth all their works.
Self intelligence effects nothing.
Con moto. = 104.
All in unison.
mf
cres.
No king is saved by the mul - ti-tude of a host; a he - ro is not de -
Con 8vi.
f
liv- ered by great- ness of strength. A lie is the horse,........ for sal -
cres.
rall.
va - tion; and by the great - ness of his strength he will not de - liv - er.
They are saved who trust in the Lord.
A tempo primo. = 112.
The women.
All.
p
Be-hold, the eye of the Lord is up - on them that fear Him; to
mf
them that wait for His mer - cy. To de - liv - er from
Con 8vi.

PSALM XXXIV.

Celebration and Worship of the Lord, for the New Church in place of the Former. The Church totally devastated and its Rejection.

PSALM XXXIV. Continued.

Celebration of the Lord because He liberates from all evil those who trust in Him.

Of David; when he changed his mind before Abimelech,
and he drove him away, and he went.

PSALM XXXV.

The Combats of the Lord with the Hells, and His Victory over them, or the Subjugation of them. The Passion of the Cross, and the Rejection of the Lord by the Church. Celebration and Worship of the Lord.

The combats of the Lord against the hells and the subjugation and prostration of them.

Of David.

Strive, O Lord, with them that strive...... with me;

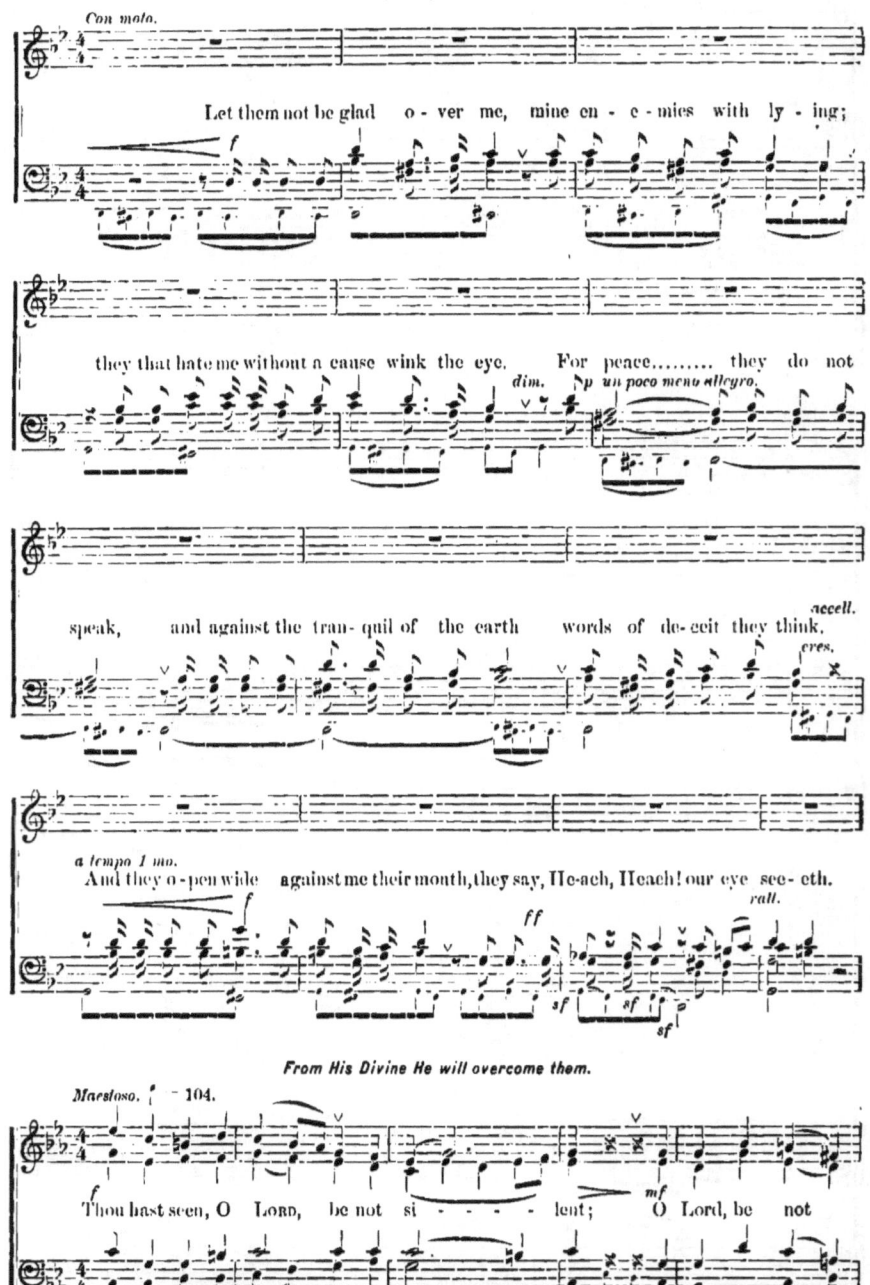

Thence the justice of the Lord will be celebrated.

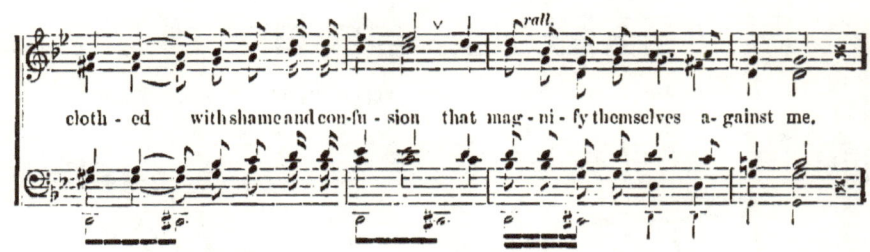

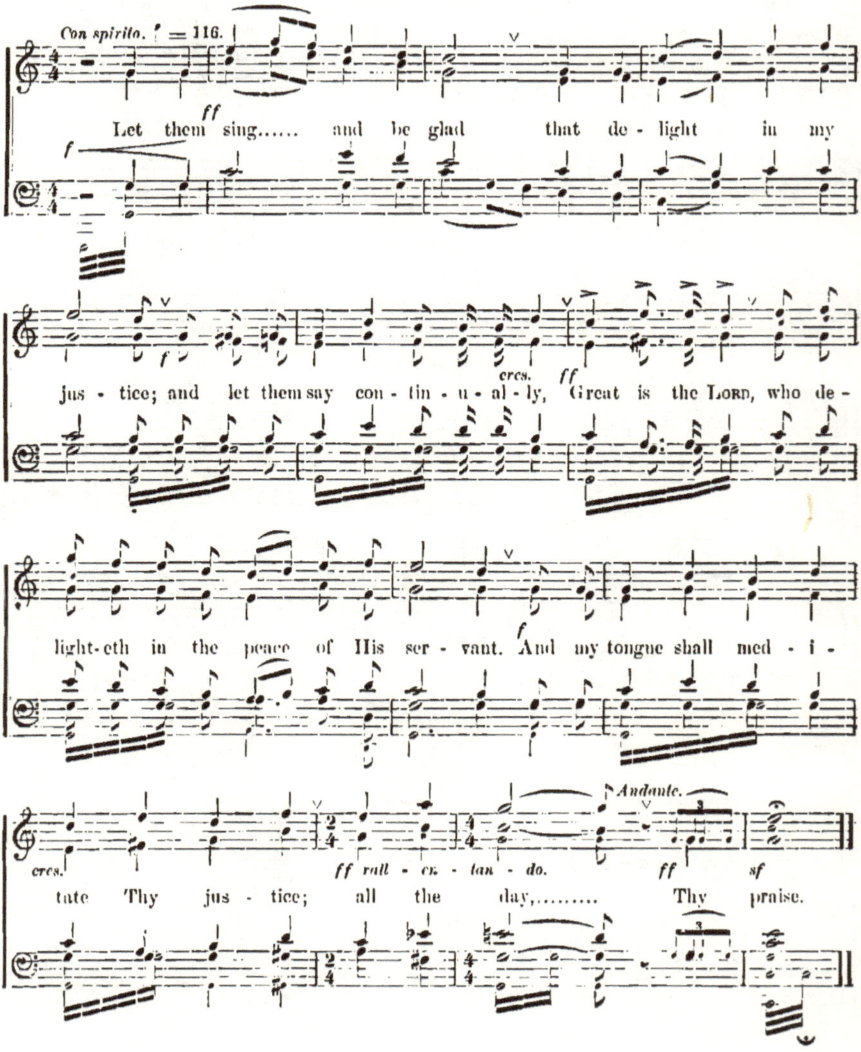

193

PSALM XXXVI.

The Rejection of the Lord by the Church. Celebration and Worship of the Lord. Redemption and Salvation by Him.

Hypocrites think evil.

Of the Conqueror; of the Servant of the Lord; of David.

A saying of transgression with the wicked, In the midst of my heart, there is no fear of God before his eyes. For he flattereth himself in his own eyes, to find his iniquity,

PSALM XXXVII.

𝔗𝔥𝔢 𝔈𝔥𝔲𝔯𝔠𝔥 𝔱𝔬𝔱𝔞𝔩𝔩𝔶 𝔡𝔢𝔳𝔞𝔰𝔱𝔞𝔱𝔢𝔡 𝔞𝔫𝔡 𝔦𝔱𝔰 𝔑𝔢𝔧𝔢𝔠𝔱𝔦𝔬𝔫. 𝔗𝔥𝔢 𝔙𝔦𝔠𝔱𝔬𝔯𝔶 𝔬𝔣 𝔱𝔥𝔢 𝔏𝔬𝔯𝔡 𝔬𝔳𝔢𝔯 𝔱𝔥𝔢 𝔥𝔢𝔩𝔩𝔰. 𝔗𝔥𝔢 𝔑𝔢𝔴 𝔈𝔥𝔲𝔯𝔠𝔥 𝔦𝔫 𝔭𝔩𝔞𝔠𝔢 𝔬𝔣 𝔱𝔥𝔢 𝔉𝔬𝔯𝔪𝔢𝔯. 𝔗𝔥𝔢 𝔏𝔞𝔰𝔱 𝔍𝔲𝔡𝔤𝔪𝔢𝔫𝔱 𝔟𝔶 𝔱𝔥𝔢 𝔏𝔬𝔯𝔡. 𝔑𝔢𝔡𝔢𝔪𝔭𝔱𝔦𝔬𝔫 𝔞𝔫𝔡 𝔖𝔞𝔩𝔳𝔞𝔱𝔦𝔬𝔫 𝔟𝔶 𝔥𝔦𝔪.

PSALM XXXVII. *Continued.*

A comparison between the lot of the evil, and the lot of the good.

The evil, although they flourish for a short time, will nevertheless perish and be cast into hell; but the good are saved by the Lord and elevated into heaven.

Of David.

Fret not thy-self be-cause of e-vil do - ers, nei-ther be thou en-vious of the work-ers of in - i - qui-ty. For like the grass they shall be sud-den-ly cut off, and as the green of the

PSALM XXXVII. *Continued.*

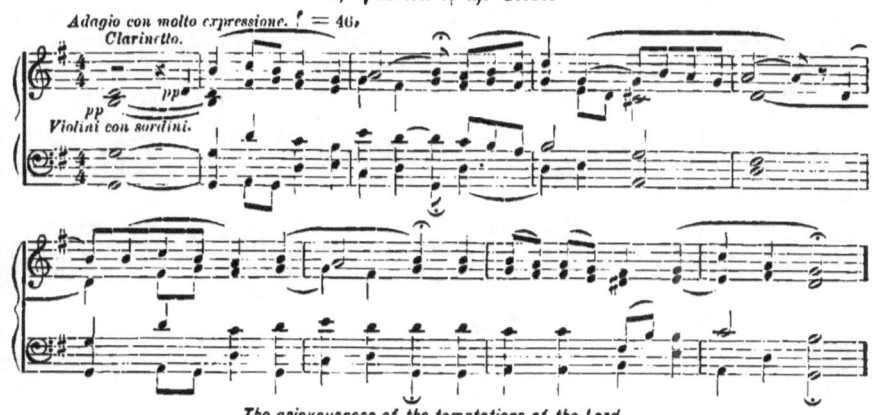

The Temptations of the Lord even to Despair, and The Passion of the Cross.

Adagio con molto expressione. = 46.
Clarinetto.
pp
pp
Violini con sordini.

The grievousness of the temptations of the Lord.

A Psalm; of David; to bring to remembrance.

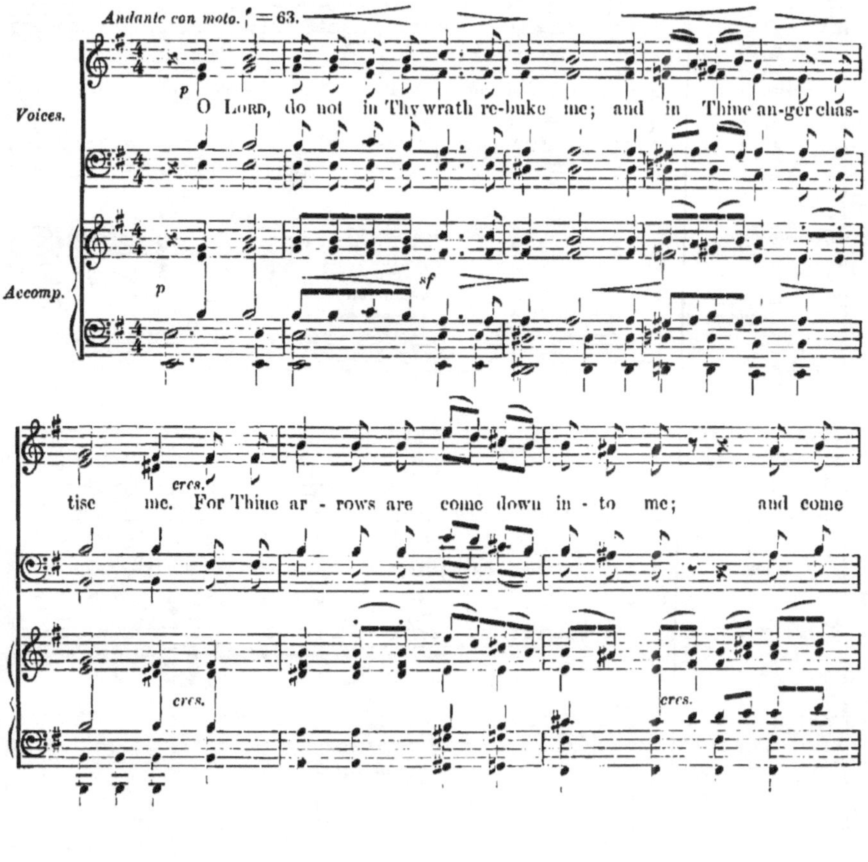
Andante con moto. = 63.
Voices.
Accomp.
p
sf
cres.
O Lord, do not in Thy wrath re-buke me; and in Thine an-ger chastise me. For Thine ar - rows are come down in - to me; and come

PSALM XXXVIII. Continued.

His trust in the Father that the hells will not prevail.

PSALM XXXIX.

The endurance of the Lord in the state of temptations.

Of the Conqueror; of Jeduthun; a Psalm; of David.

He wished for the end of them.

The endurance of the Lord in the state of temptations.

PSALM XXXIX. Concluded.

Prayer to the Father that He be not forsaken.

PSALM XL.

The State of the Lord's Humiliation before the Father. The New Church in place of the Former. The Passion of the Cross. Celebration and Worship of the Lord.

Thanksgiving and celebration of the Father because He has helped Him.

Of the Conqueror; of David; a Psalm.

I wait-ed for the Lord; and He in-clin-ed un-to me, and heard my

And let those rejoice in the Lord, who worship Him.

PSALM XL. *Concluded.*

Trust from His Divine, against those who intend death to Him.

PSALM XLI.

The Temptations of the Lord in general. The Rejection of the Lord by the Church. His Victory over the Hells.

He that is in temptations and thence in affliction, will always be sustained and thereby vivified.

Of the Conqueror; a Psalm; of David.

Hap - py is he that con - sid - er - eth the

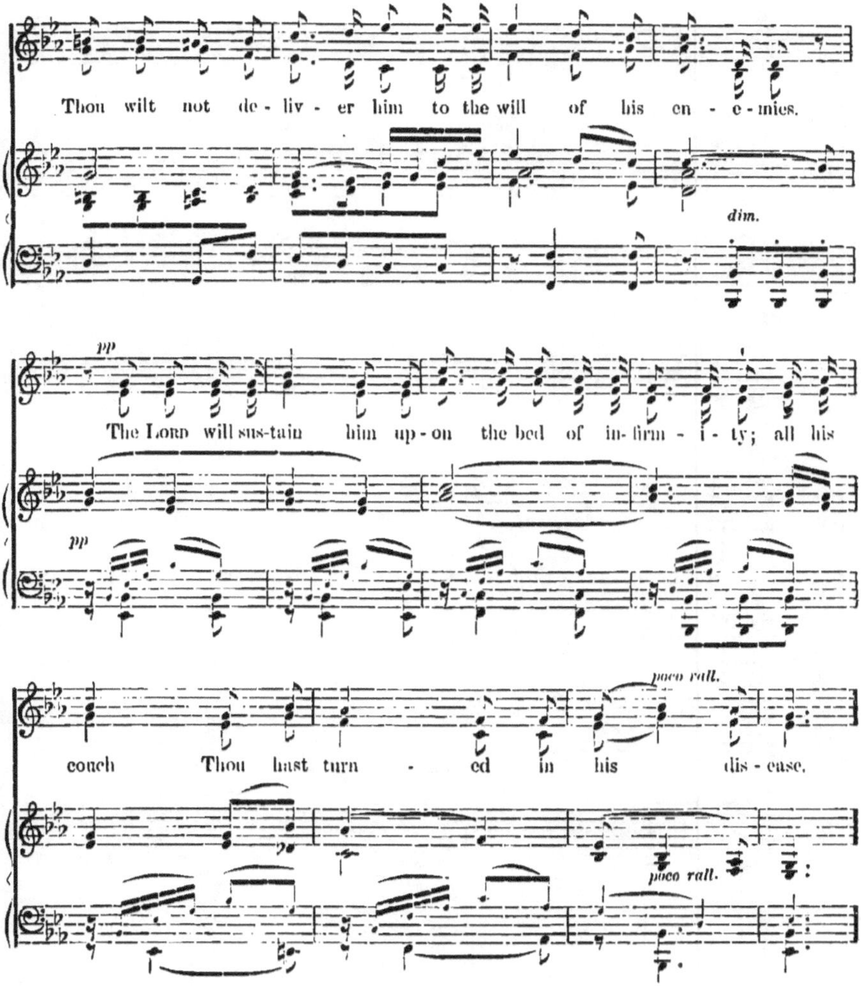

The hells devise evils among themselves, against the Lord.

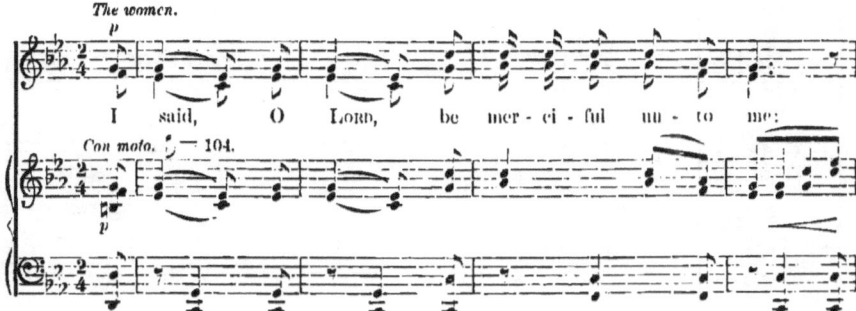

The Lord has integrity.

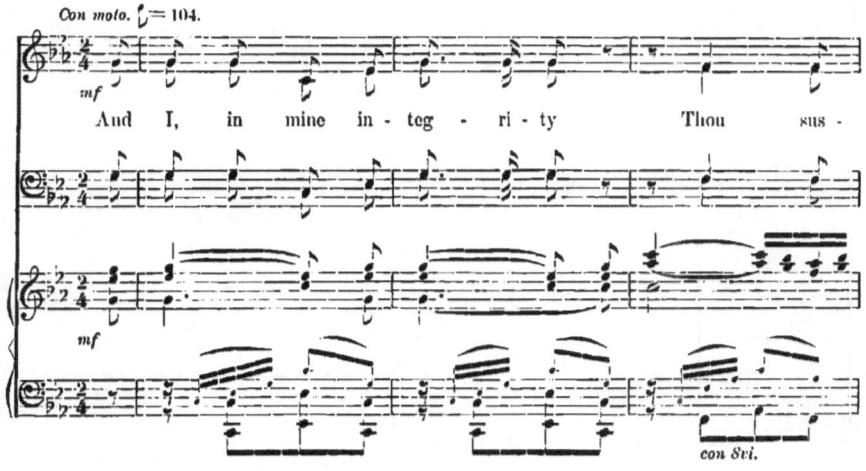

266   PSALM XLI. *Concluded.*

PSALM XLII.

The Temptations of the Lord even to Despair.
His Victory over the Hells, or the Subjugation of them.

PSALM XLII. *Continuea.*

The state of the Lord's grief and perturbation from temptations, with trust from the Divine.

Of the Conqueror; making intelligent; of the sons of Korah.

As the hart cri-eth out for streams of wa-ters,

sempre con 8vi.

so my soul cri-eth out un-to Thee, O God. Thirst-eth my

soul for God, the liv - ing God;...... when shall I come that

PSALM XLIII.

**The Temptations of the Lord even to Despair.
The State of His Humiliation before the Father.**

PSALM XLIII. *Continued.*

The grievousness of the temptations of the Lord even to despair.

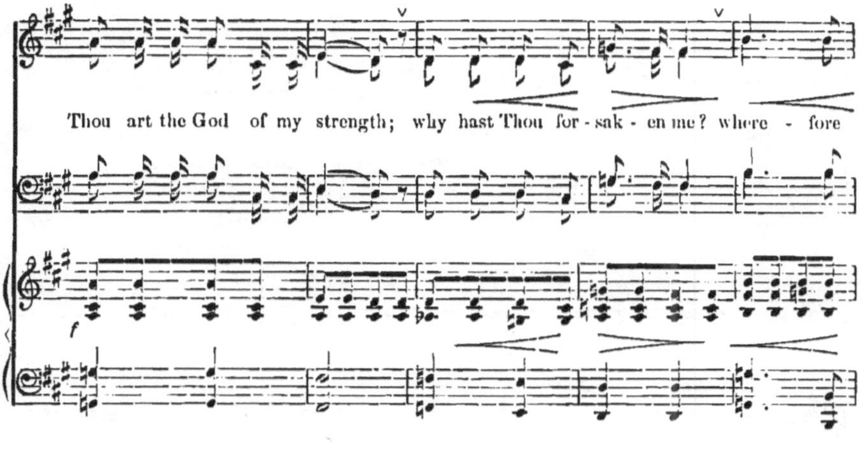
Thou art the God of my strength; why hast Thou for-sak-en me? where-fore
f

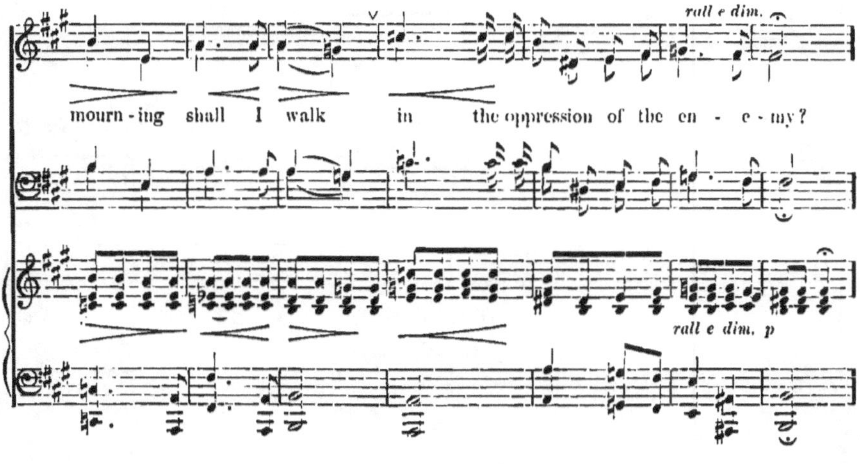
rall e dim.
mourn-ing shall I walk in the oppression of the en-e-my?
rall e dim. p

Prayer to the Father that the Divine Truth may comfort Him.

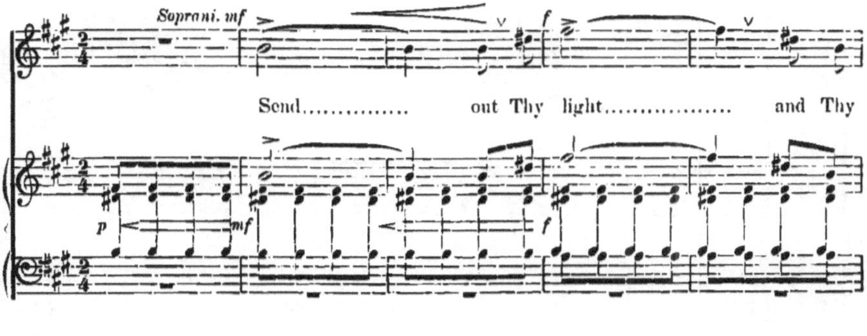
Soprani. mf
f
Send............... out Thy light.................. and Thy
p
mf
f

PSALM XLIV.

The New Church in place of the Former. The successive Vastation of the Church. The Church totally devastated and its Rejection. The Temptations of the Lord even to Despair. The Glorification of the Human of the Lord.

The Church was established by the Lord with the ancients, the evil being cast out.

Of the Conqueror; of the Sons of Korah; making intelligent.

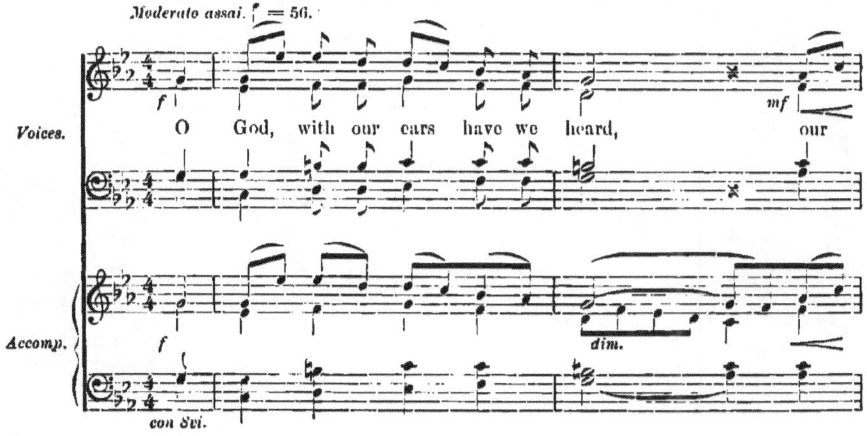

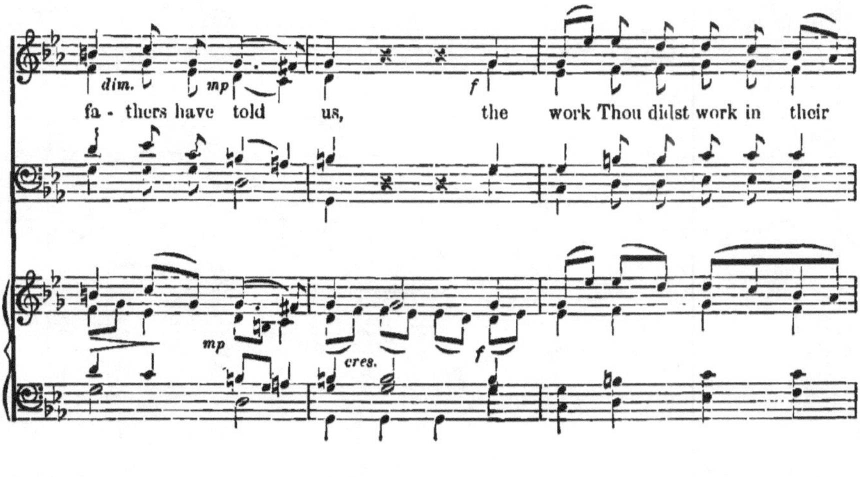

Voices. O God, with our ears have we heard, our fa-thers have told us, the work Thou didst work in their

Accomp.

PSALM XLIV. *Continued.*

This was done by God and not by man.

Nevertheless the hells now prevail over Him, as if there were no Divine Presence; whence it is that there is no church.

PSALM XLIV. *Continued.*

He is blasphemed by the evil within the church.

PSALM XLIV. *Continued.*

He suffers this for the sake of the Divine.

Prayer that the Divine may therefore bring help.

He is in the extreme state of temptations, as if He were forsaken.

PSALM XLV.

Celebration and Worship of the Lord. His Victory over the Hells. The Glorification of His Human. The New Church and the New Heaven.

Maestoso.
ff

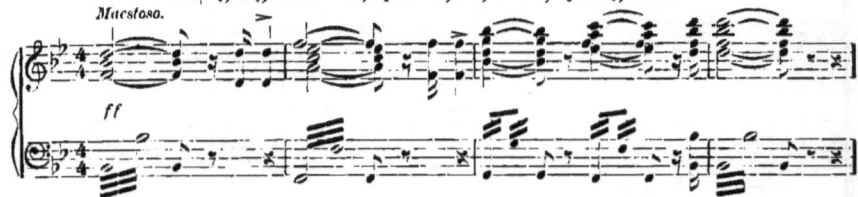

A magnificent word concerning the Lord, and conjunction with Him.

The Divine Truth is His alone, by which He has powerfully conquered the hells, and made His Human Divine. Hence are the affections of truth in which the societies of heaven are.

Of the Conqueror; upon Shoshanim; of the sons of Korah;
making intelligent; a song of loves.

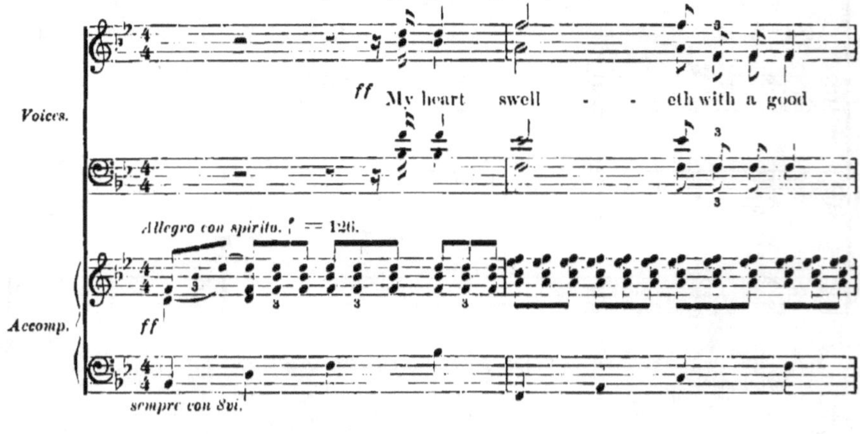
Voices.
ff My heart swell - - eth with a good
Allegro con spirito. ♩ = 126.
Accomp.
ff
sempre con 8vi.

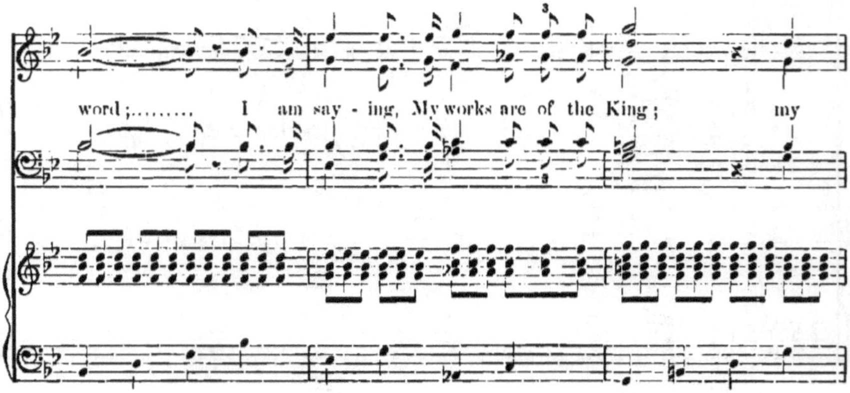
word;......... I am say - ing, My works are of the King; my

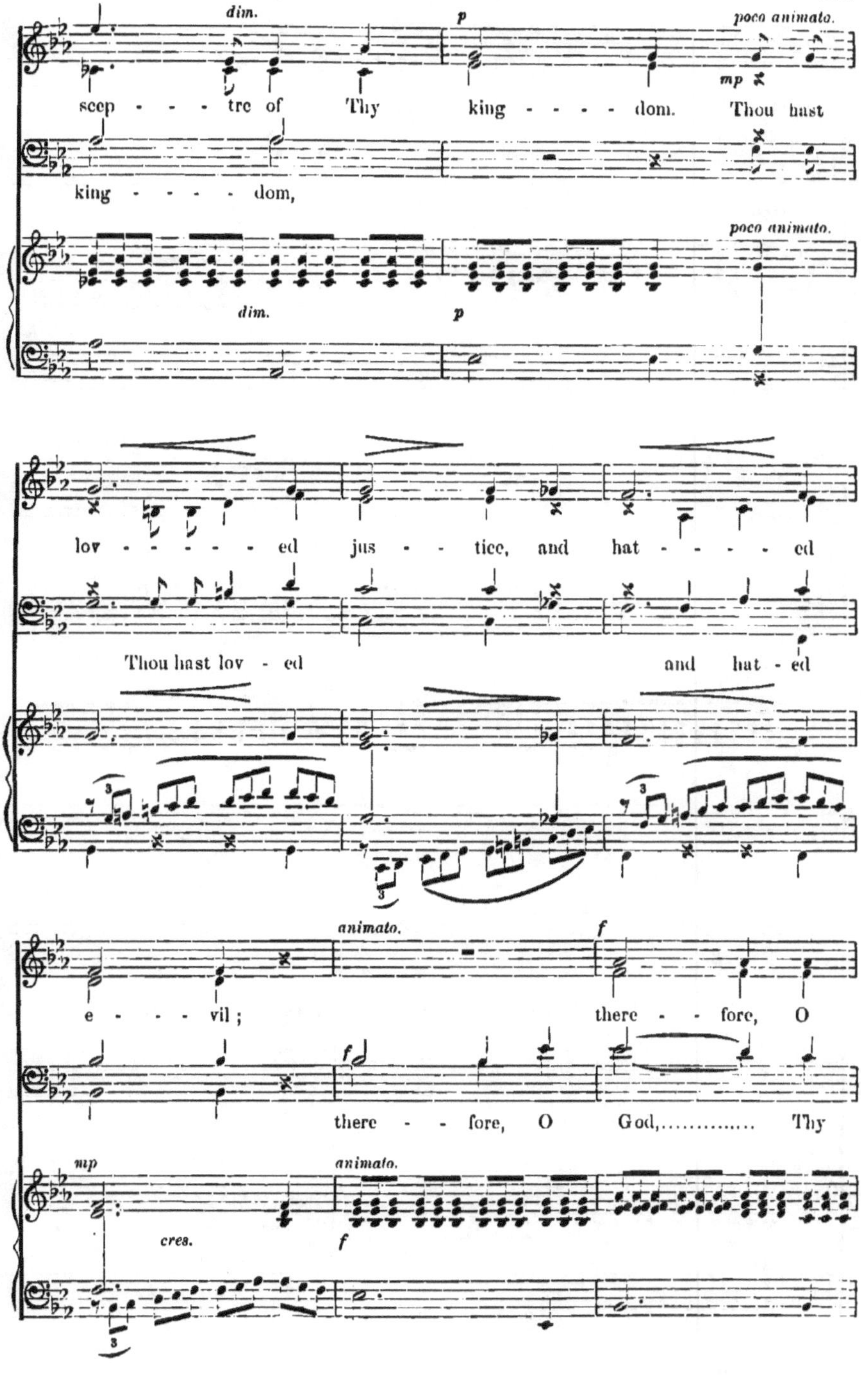
dim.
p
poco animato.
mp
scep - - - tre of Thy king - - - - - dom. Thou hast
king - - - - dom,
poco animato.
dim.
p
lov - - - - - - ed jus - - tice, and hat - - - - - ed
Thou hast lov - ed and hat - ed
animato.
f
e - - - vil; there - - fore, O
f
there - - fore, O God,............ Thy
mp
animato.
cres.
f

PSALM XLV. *Continued.* 309

The church, where the Word is, should recede from the affections of the natural man. Thus it will be the church of the Lord, and will have the knowledges of truth and good, with sciences subservient. Then there will be conjunction with the Lord in heaven, and the whole church will serve Him.

PSALM XLV. *Continued.* 313

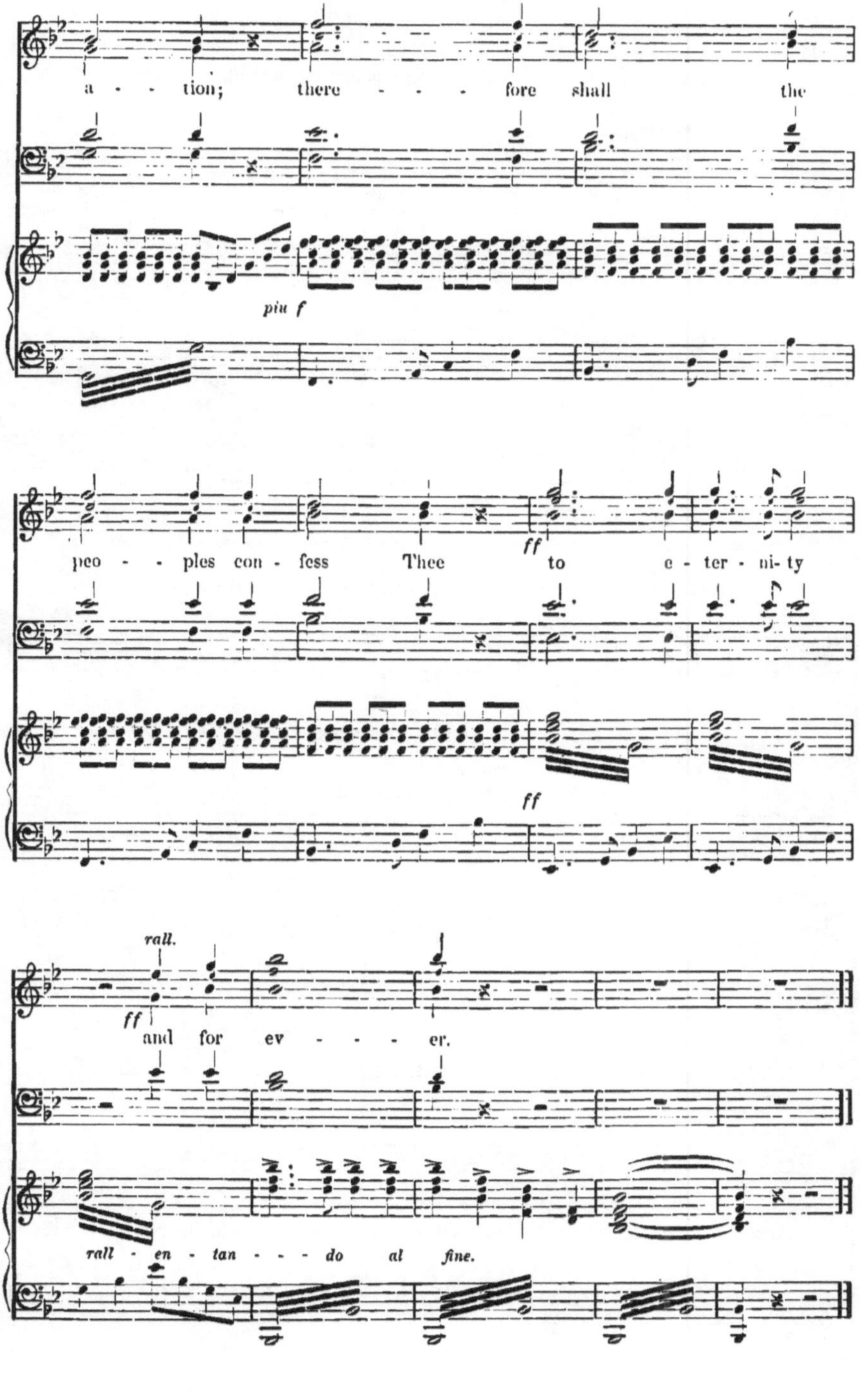
a - - tion; there - - - - fore shall the
piu f
peo - - ples con - fess Thee to e - ter - ni- ty
ff
ff
rall.
ff
and for ev - - - - er.
rall - en - tan - - - do al fine.

PSALM XLVI.

The Last Judgment by the Lord. Redemption and Salvation by Him.

Andante tranquillo ♩ = 66.
pp
p
cres.
mf
p rall e dim. pp

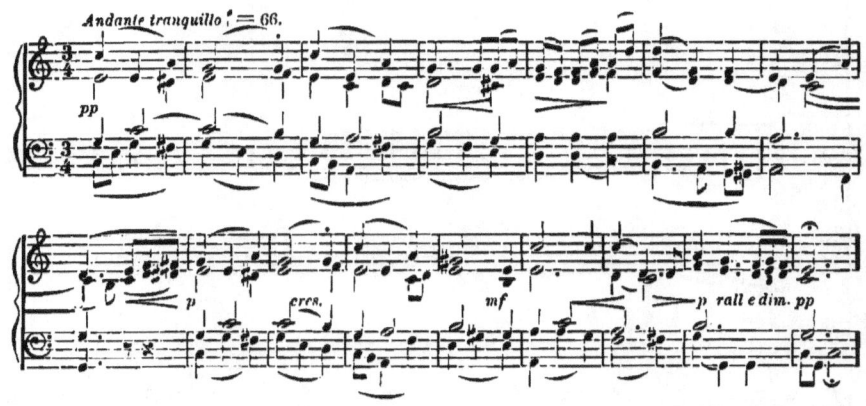

There will be protection from the Lord, when the last judgment comes and while it continues.

Of the Conqueror; of the sons of Korah; upon Alamoth; a Song.

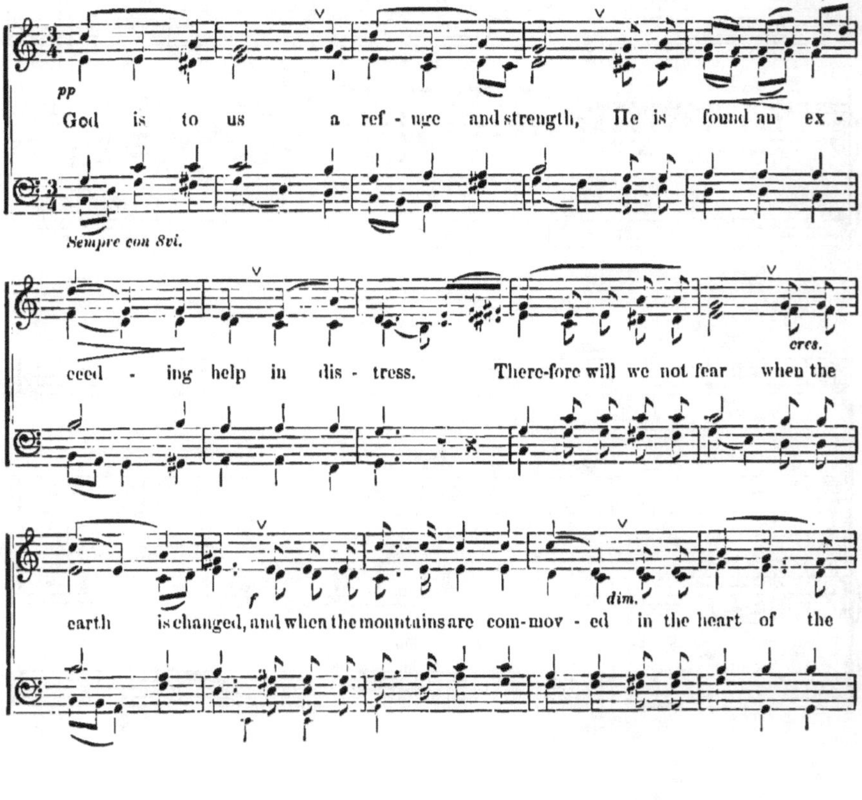
pp
God is to us a ref - uge and strength, He is found an ex -
Sempre con 8vi.
ceed - ing help in dis - tress. There-fore will we not fear when the
cres.
earth is changed, and when the mountains are com-mov - ed in the heart of the
f
dim.

They who are of the church and in the doctrine of truth, will be saved by the Lord when He comes.

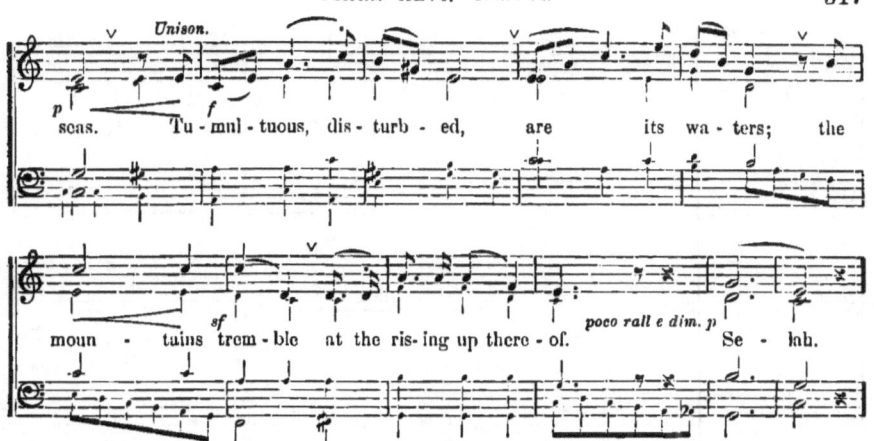

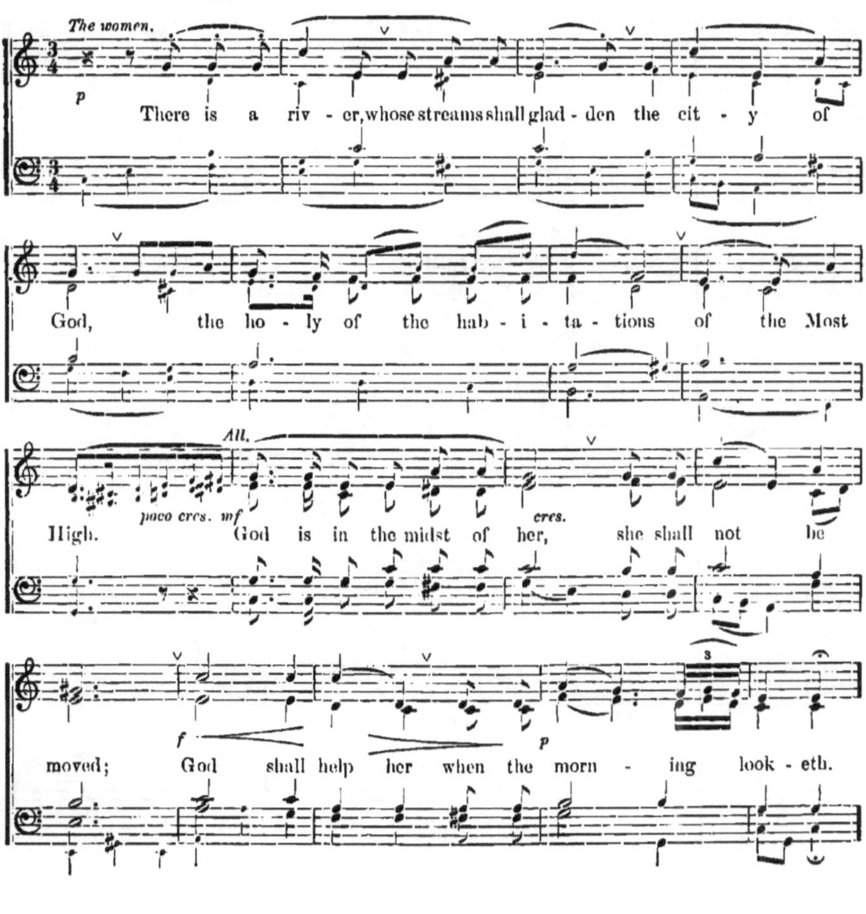

There will be protection from the Lord, when the last judgment comes and while it continues.

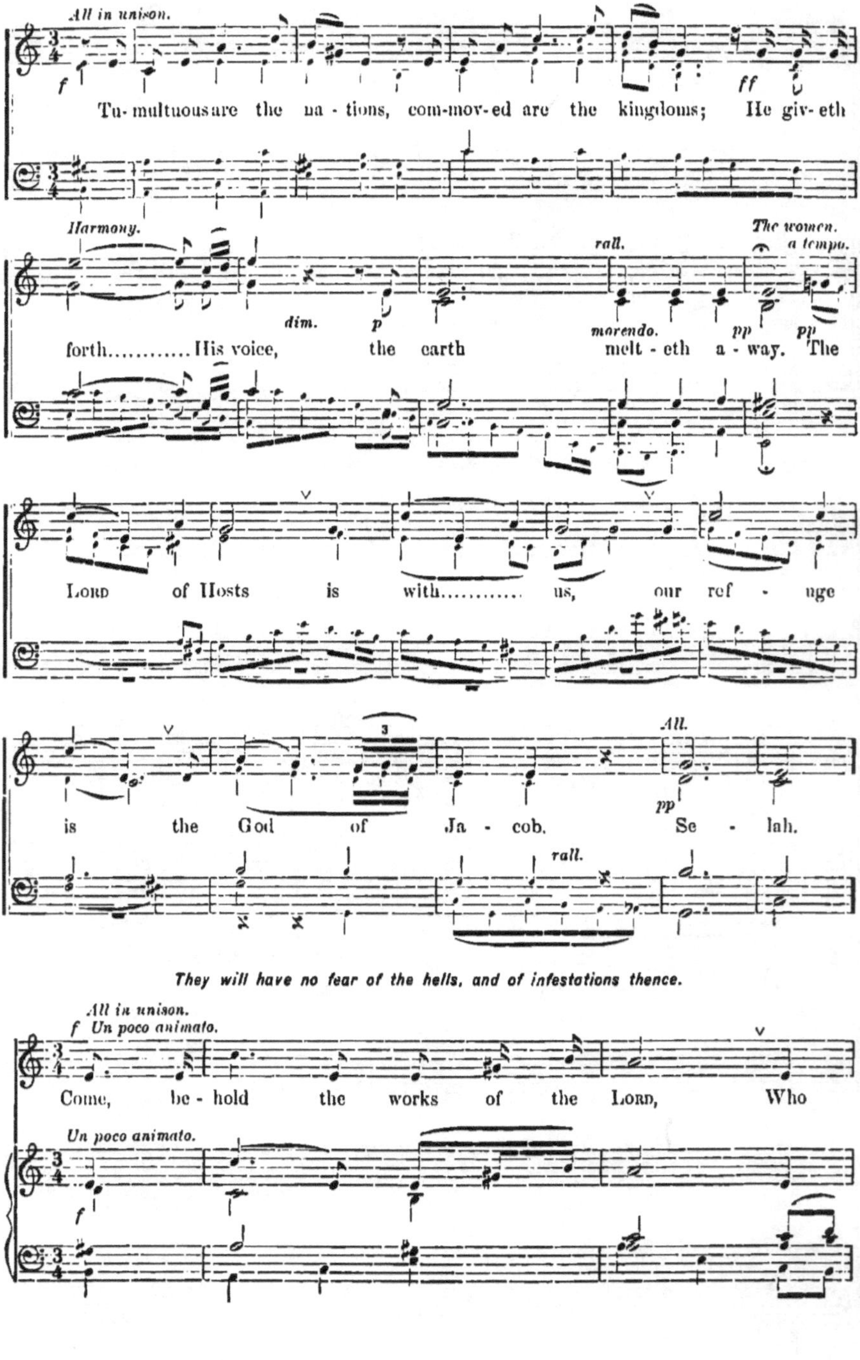
All in unison.
Tu-multuous are the na-tions, com-mov-ed are the kingdoms; He giv-eth
Harmony.
dim. p
rall.
morendo.
pp pp
The women. a tempo.
forth............His voice, the earth melt-eth a-way. The
LORD of Hosts is with............ us, our ref-uge
All.
is the God of Ja-cob. Se-lah.
rall.
They will have no fear of the hells, and of infestations thence.
All in unison.
f Un poco animato.
Come, be-hold the works of the LORD, Who
Un poco animato.

This is from the Lord.

PSALM XLVII.

**Celebration and Worship of the Lord. The New Church in place of the Former.
The New Church and at the same time the New Heaven.**

Celebration of the Lord because He reigns over the church.

Of the Conqueror; of the Sons of Korah; a Psalm.

All ye peo — ples, clap with the hand; sing un-to

PSALM XLVII. Continued.

He will remove falses and evils.

He will establish the church, and will therefore be celebrated.

PSALM XLVIII.

The New Church and at the same time the New Heaven. The Temptations of the Lord even to Despair. The Glorification of His Human. The Advent of the Lord. Celebration and Worship of Him.

Of the spiritual kingdom of the Lord, how admirable!

A Song; a Psalm; of the sons of Korah.

Great is the LORD, and prais-ed ex-ceed-ing-ly, in the cit-y of our God...... the mountain of His ho-li-ness.

PSALM XLVIII. Continued.

Beau-ti-ful in sit-u-a-tion, the joy of all the earth, the
Beau-ti-ful in sit-u-a-tion, the joy of all the
moun-tain of Zi - on, the sides of the north the
earth, the mountain of Zi - on, the sides of the north,
cit - y of.......... the great King.
God, in her pal-a-ces is known as a ref-uge.

He will dissipate all falses.

The men. For, be-hold, the kings were as-sem-bled, they pass-ed by to-
geth-er. They saw, so were they as-ton-ish-ed;

It is the Divine Human.

Thence are all things of heaven and the church.

PSALM XLIX.

The Successive Vastation of the Church. The Last Judgment by the Lord. Redemption and Salvation by Him.

An exhortation to attend to what follows.
Of the Conqueror; of the Sons of Korah; a Psalm.

Hear this,............ all ye peo - ple; give ear, all ye in - hab - it - ants of the world. Both the sons of men and the

PSALM XLIX. *Continued.*

Of those who are merely natural, and glory from scientifics and from their own intelligence.

There is no salvation thence; thus, notwithstanding they glory in these things, they will nevertheless perish.

PSALM L.

The Lord's Advent. The Last Judgment by Him. The Successive Vastation of the Church.

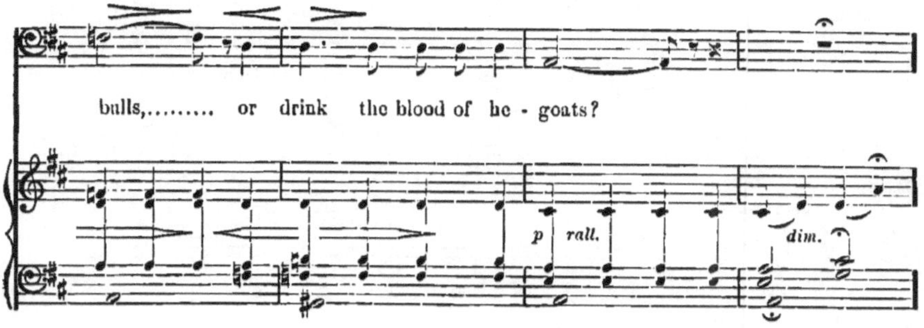

349

bulls,......... or drink the blood of he-goats?

But He desires confession of the heart.

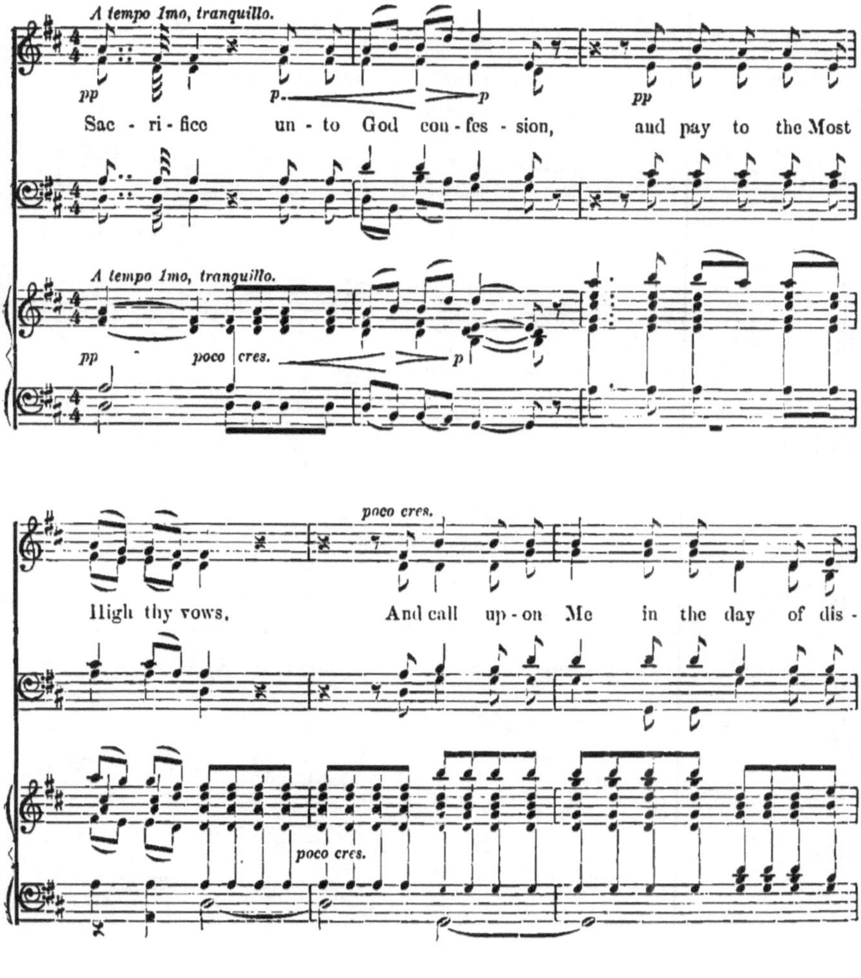

A tempo 1mo, tranquillo.

Sac-ri-fice un-to God con-fes-sion, and pay to the Most High thy vows, And call up-on Me in the day of dis-

External worship effects nothing when evils are committed.
They do these and therefore evil will overtake them.

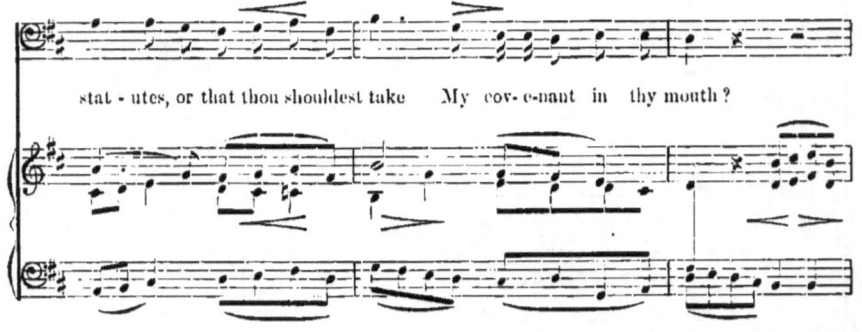

PSALM L. *Concluded.*

The Lord desires confession of the heart.

PSALM V: 8.

PSALM CXXII: 6. 7.

Joy of the Lord over the New Church where He reigns.

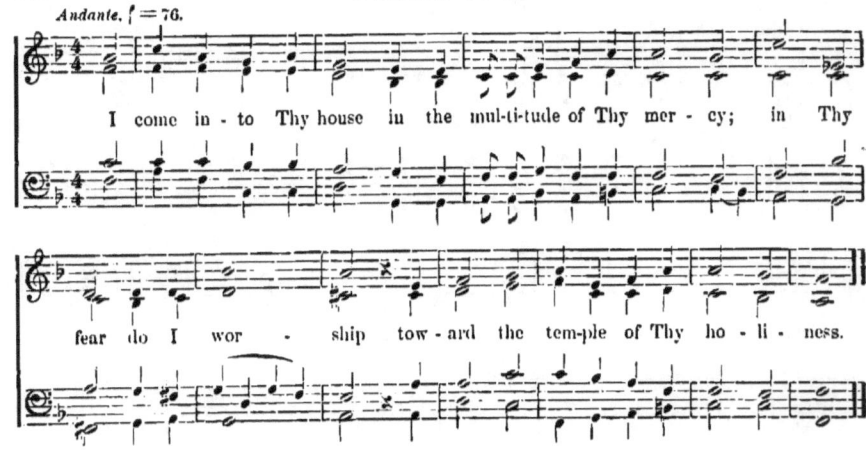

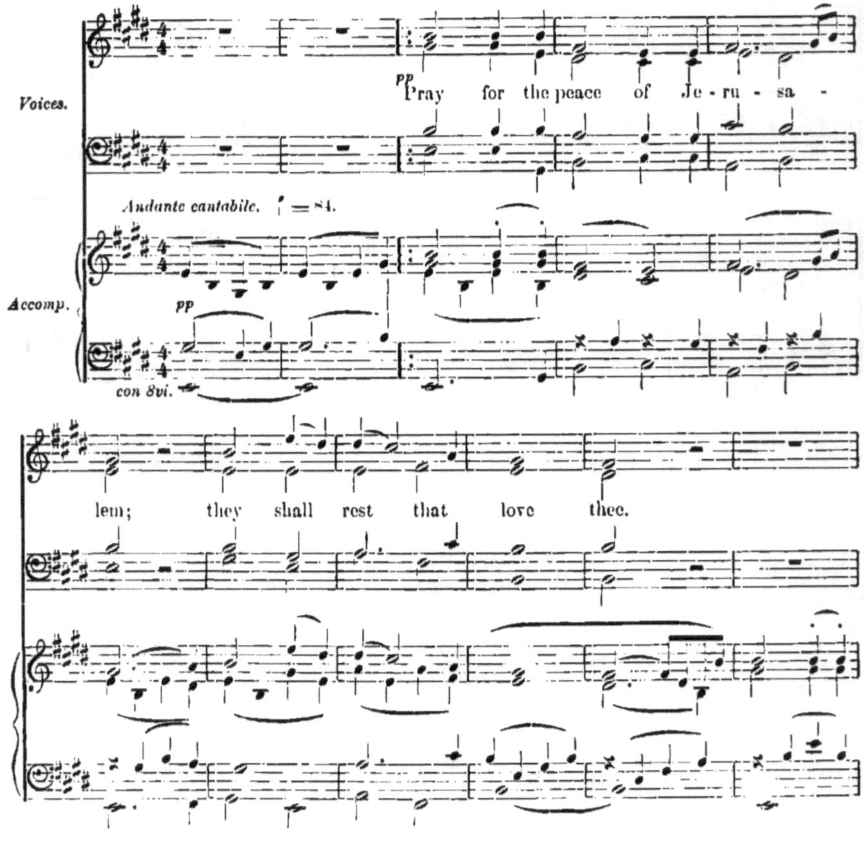

ISAIAH VI: 3.

JOHN III: 8.

The Lord by His Divine Truth gives man new life, but man does not know, from any perception in himself, how it is done.

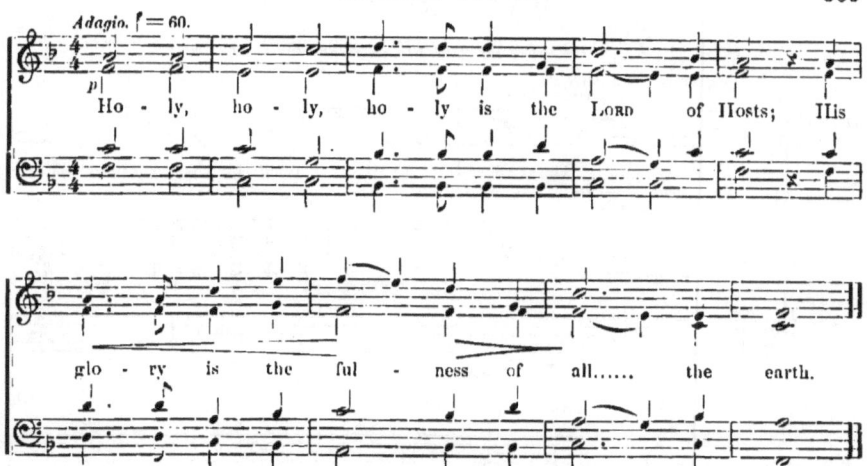

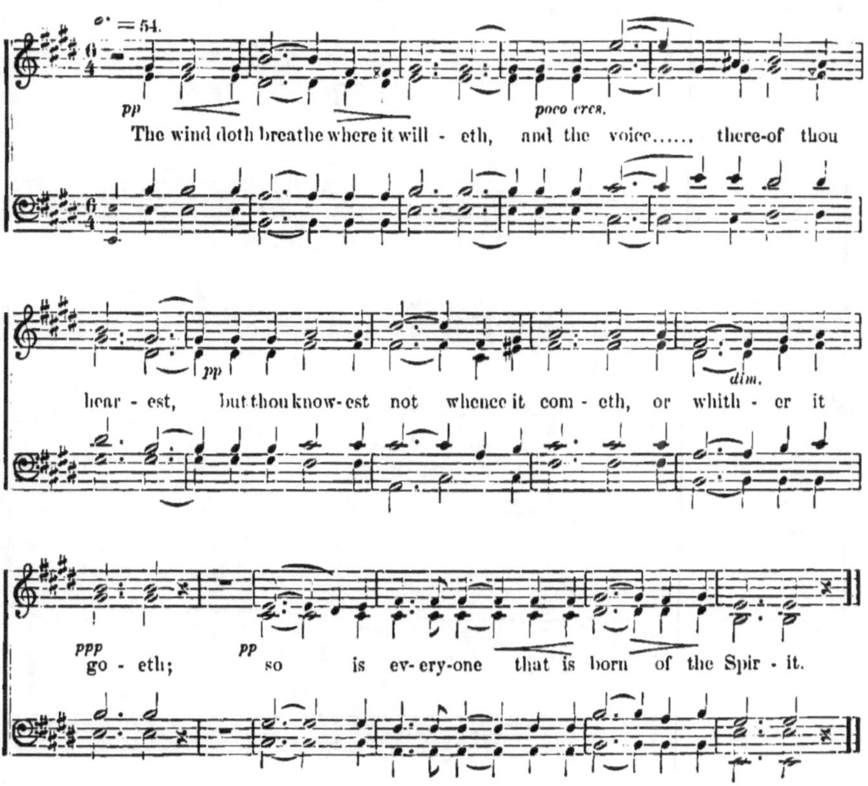

ISAIAH XL: 3–5.

The advent of the Lord, when the good will be saved, and the evil perish.

PSALM CXVI: 12–14.

ISAIAH XII: 2, 3.

Confession that the Lord from Divine Power will save the human race.

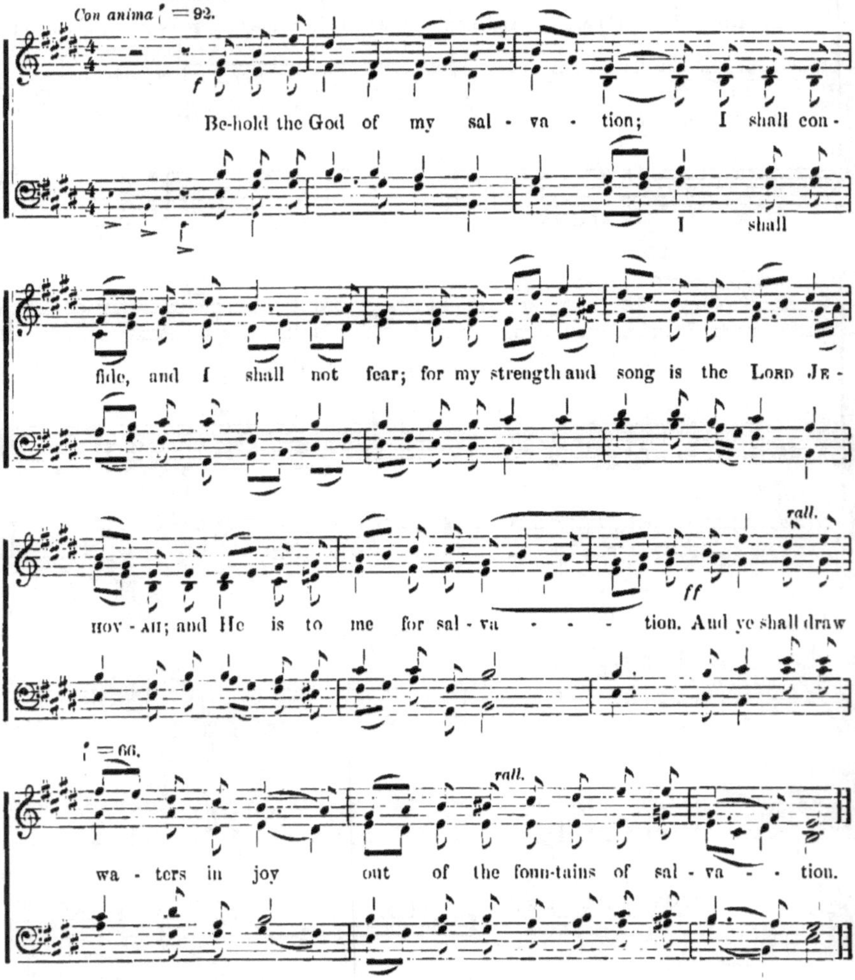

Con anima ♩ = 92.

Be-hold the God of my sal-va-tion; I shall con-fide, and I shall not fear; for my strength and song is the LORD JE-HOV-AH; and He is to me for sal-va-tion. And ye shall draw wa-ters in joy out of the foun-tains of sal-va-tion.

♩ = 66.

HABAKKUK II: 20.

Largo ♩ = 66.

The LORD is in the temple of His ho-li-ness; be si-lent be-fore Him, all the earth.

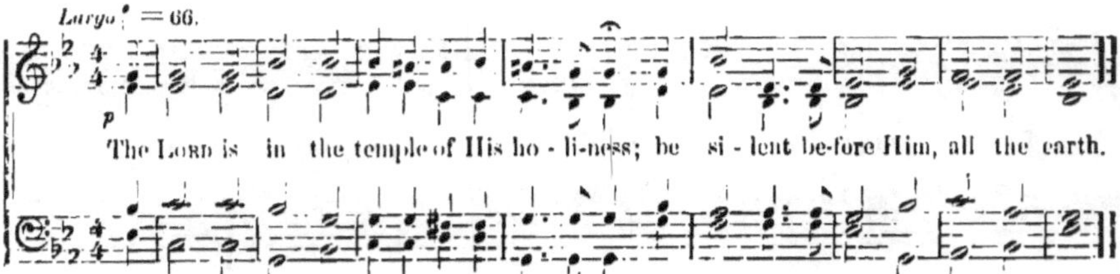

JEREMIAH XVII: 7, 8.

They that trust in the Lord will always have good and truth.

MATTHEW VII : 7, 8.

Whatsoever a man asks, not from himself, but from the Lord, is given.

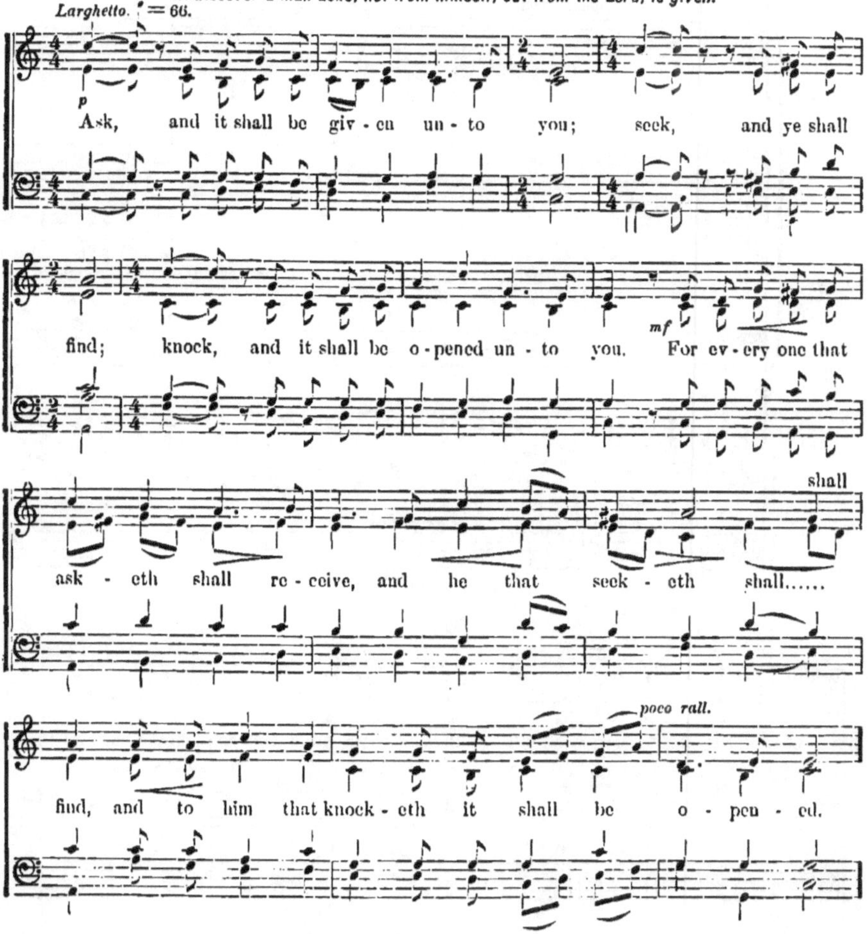

Larghetto. ♩ = 66.

Ask, and it shall be giv-en un-to you; seek, and ye shall find; knock, and it shall be o-pened un-to you. For ev-ery one that ask-eth shall re-ceive, and he that seek-eth shall...... find, and to him that knock-eth it shall be o-pen-ed.

APOCALYPSE III : 22.

Let him who understands, obey, what the Divine Truth teaches those who are to be of the New Church.

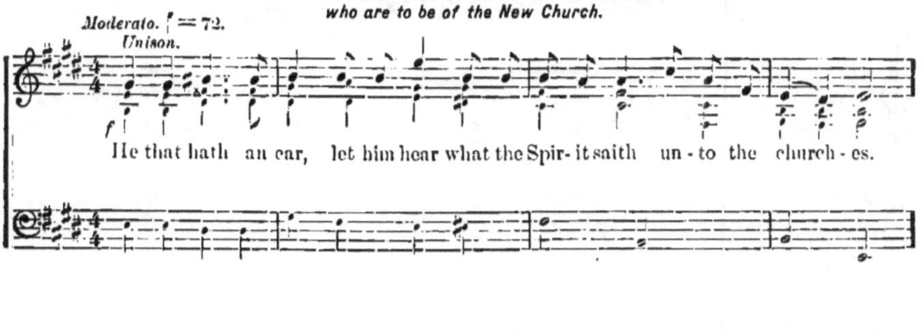

Moderato. ♩ = 72.
Unison.

He that hath an ear, let him hear what the Spir-it saith un-to the church-es.

MATTHEW XXI: 9.

The Lord be glorified, because from Him is all Divine Truth.

And the multitudes that went before, and those that followed, cried, saying:—

Allegro Moderato. ♩ = 92.

1st Choir. Ho-san-na to the Son of Da-vid; bless-ed is He that com-eth in the name of the Lord; in the name of the

2d Choir. Ho-san-na to the Son of Da-vid; bless-ed is He that com-eth in the name of the

Accomp.

JOHN IV: 13, 14, 15. *Concluded.*

JOHN IV: 23–24.

The Lord, by His Divine Truth, inflows into and illustrates all who receive Him.

JOHN IV: 23, 24. *Concluded.*

such to worship Him. God is a Spirit, and they that worship Him must worship in spirit and in truth.

MATTHEW XI: 28–30.

If a man interiorly acknowledges the Lord, and resists the evils that are with him, the way to heaven is not difficult; for then he is led by the Lord, and not by himself, and the Lord resists and removes the evils.

Andante. ♩ = 72.

Come unto Me,...... all ye that labor and are burdened, and I will revive...... you. Take My yoke upon you, and learn of Me, that I am meek and humble in heart, and ye shall find rest for your souls. For My yoke is easy and My burden light.

JOHN V : 39.

The Lord testifies in His Word concerning Himself.

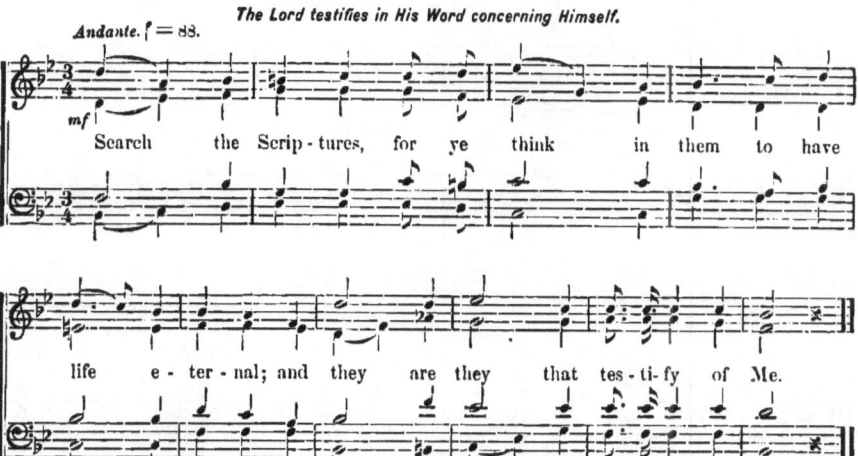

Andante. ♩ = 88.
mf
Search the Scrip - tures, for ye think in them to have
life e - ter - nal; and they are they that tes - ti - fy of Me.

APOCALYPSE XX : 6.

Felicity of eternal life, and illustration by conjunction with the Lord, to those who come into heaven.

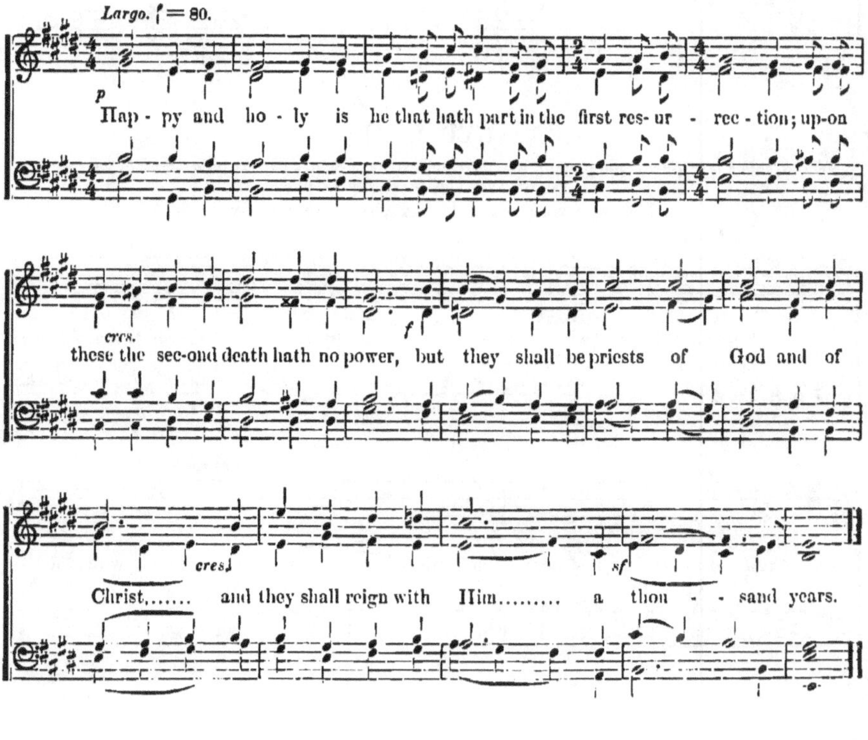

Largo. ♩ = 80.
p
Hap - py and ho - ly is he that hath part in the first res - ur - rec - tion; up-on
cres.
f
these the sec-ond death hath no power, but they shall be priests of God and of
cres.
sf
Christ,...... and they shall reign with Him......... a thou - - sand years.

JOHN XI: 25, 26.

He that acknowledges the Lord, and lives a life of charity, will not be damned, but will rise again into life eternal.

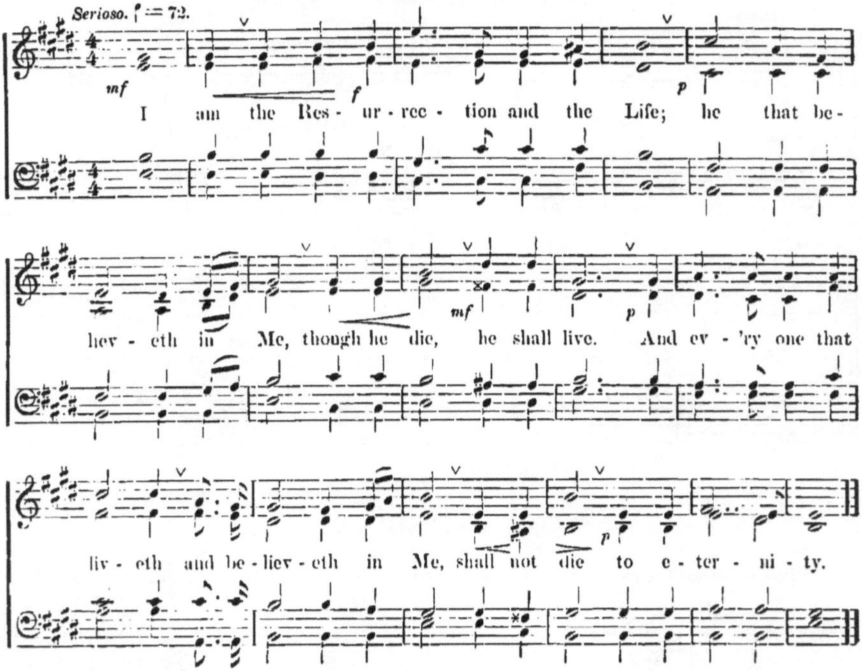
Serioso. 𝅗𝅥 = 72.
mf
f
p
I am the Res - ur - rec - tion and the Life; he that be -
mf
p
liev - eth in Me, though he die, he shall live. And ev - 'ry one that
p
liv - eth and be - liev - eth in Me, shall not die to e - ter - ni - ty.

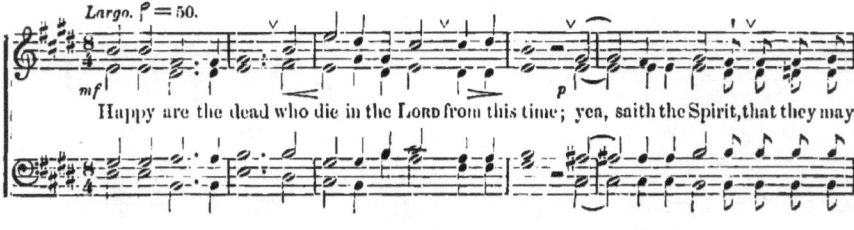

APOCALYPSE XIV: 13.

Resurrection into life eternal, of those who have suffered temptations on account of faith in the Lord and life according to His precepts.

And I heard a voice out of heaven, saying unto me, write :—

Largo. 𝅗𝅥 = 50.
mf
p
Happy are the dead who die in the Lord from this time; yea, saith the Spirit, that they may
poco rall.
f
p
rest from their la - bors, for their works do fol - low with them.

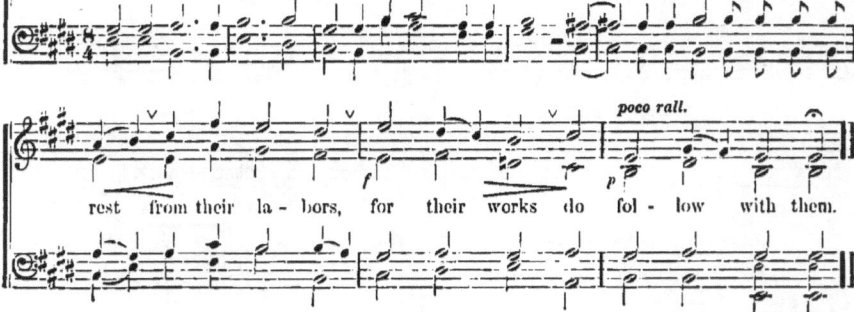

APOCALYPSE I: 4–8.

The Lord appears in His Word, and reveals Himself as the God of heaven and earth.

John to the seven Churches which are in Asia:

APOCALYPSE I: 4–8. *Continued.*

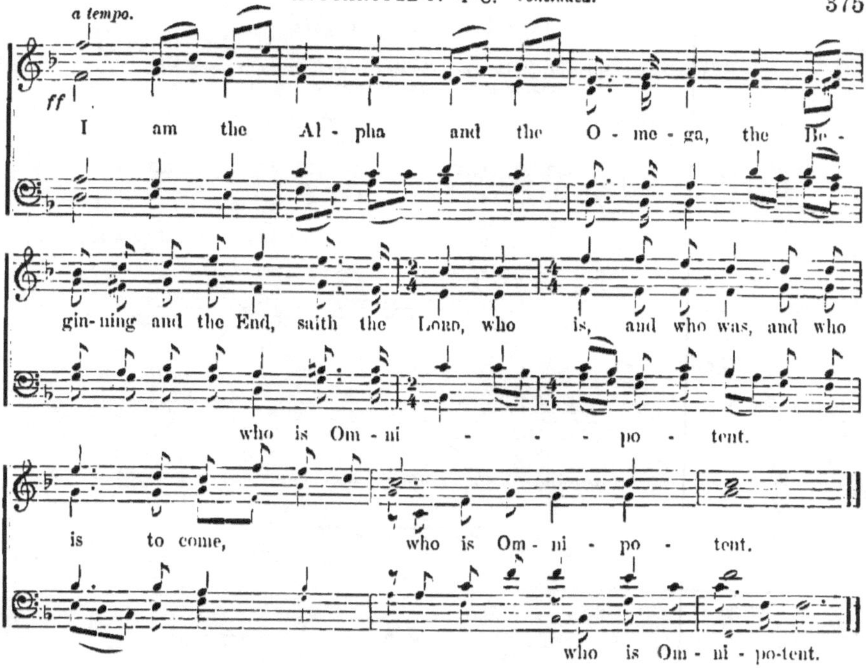

APOCALYPSE XIX: 1, 2.

Confession, that salvation is from the Lord.

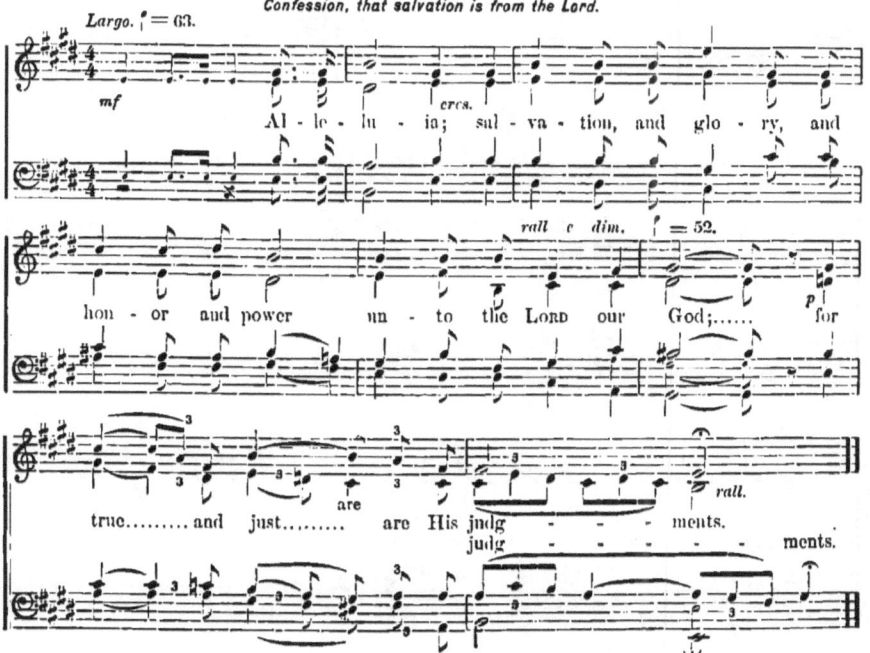

APOCALYPSE I: 17, 18.

The Lord alone is Infinite and Eternal, He alone is God, from Him alone is life, and He alone has power to save.

And He laid His right hand upon me, saying unto me:

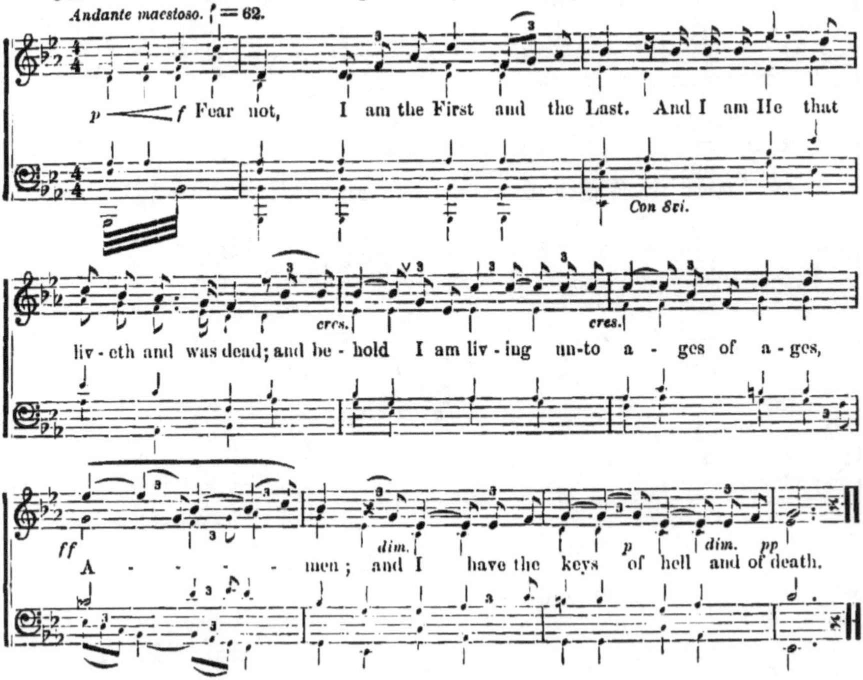

APOCALYPSE II: 7.

He who fights against the evils and falses of his natural life will enter interiorly into the truths of wisdom and of faith.

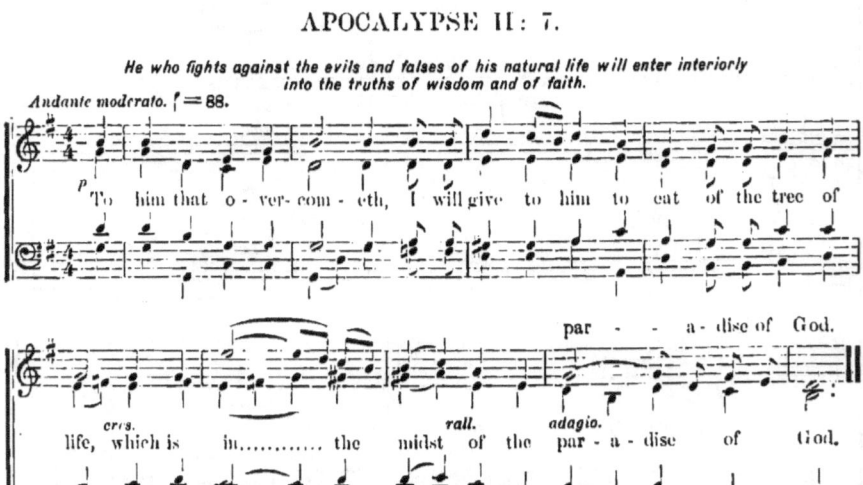

APOCALYPSE III: 20.

The Lord is perpetually present, and conjoins Himself with all who receive Him.

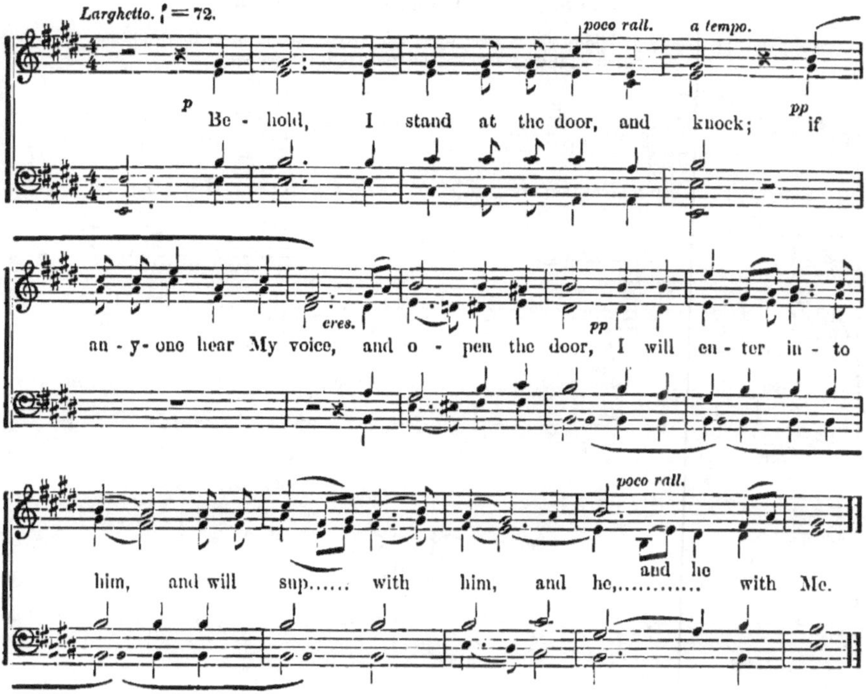
Larghetto. = 72.
poco rall.
a tempo.
p
Be - hold, I stand at the door, and knock; pp if
cres.
pp
an - y - one hear My voice, and o - pen the door, I will en - ter in - to
poco rall.
him, and will sup...... with him, and he,............ and he with Me.

APOCALYPSE V: 13.

In the Divine Human of the Lord is the all of heaven and the church.

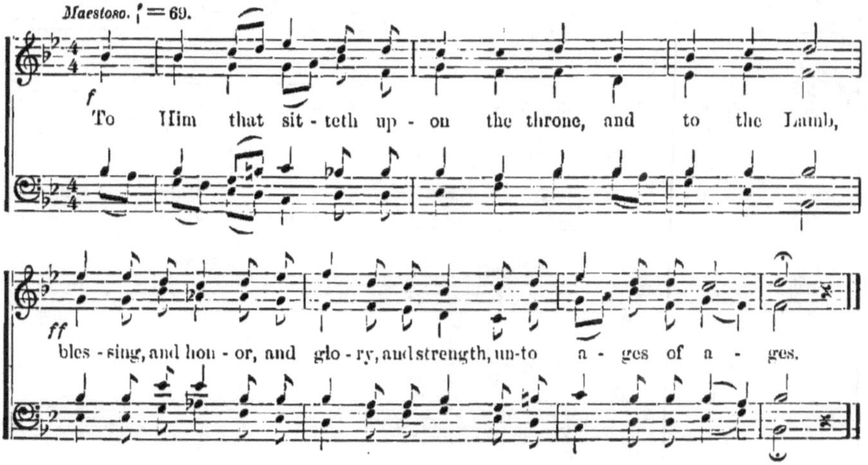
Maestoso. = 69.
f
To Him that sit - teth up - on the throne, and to the Lamb,
ff
bles - sing, and hon - or, and glo - ry, and strength, un-to a - ges of a - ges.

APOCALYPSE XI: 16, 17, 18.

Confession and glorification of the Lord by the angels of heaven. In His Human He is the God of heaven and earth; He will establish the New Church; and they who have destroyed the church will be judged and cast into hell.

And the twenty and four elders who were before God sitting upon their thrones, fell upon their faces, and adored God, saying:—

APOCALYPSE XIV: 7.

Confession that all the truth of the Word is from the Lord, according to which every man will be judged; and that the Lord alone is to be worshipped.

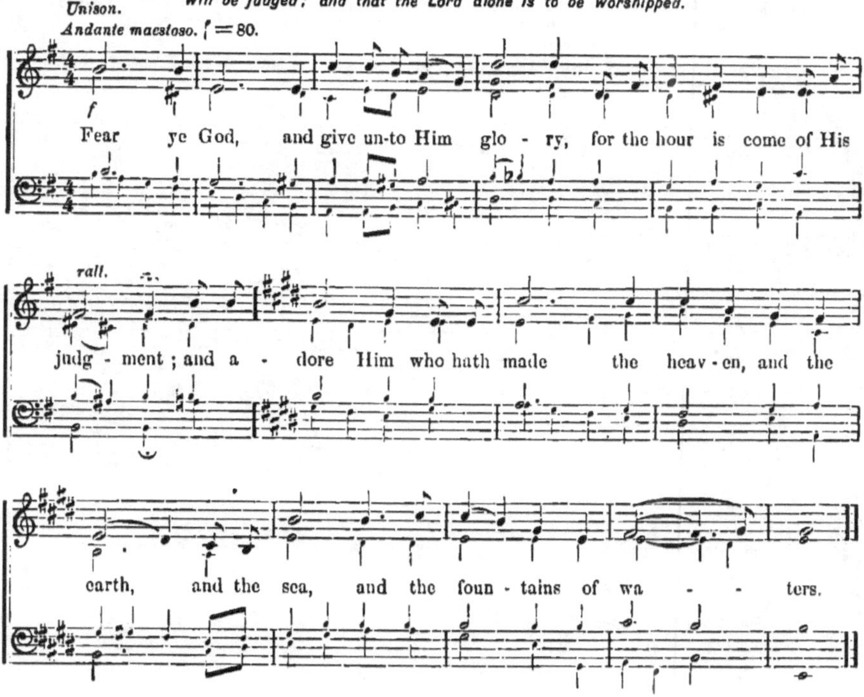
Unison.
Andante maestoso. ♩ = 80.
f
Fear ye God, and give un-to Him glo - ry, for the hour is come of His
rall.
judg - ment; and a - dore Him who hath made the heav - en, and the
earth, and the sea, and the foun - tains of wa - - ters.

MATTHEW XIX: 14.

No one can enter heaven unless he has innocence.

But Jesus said:

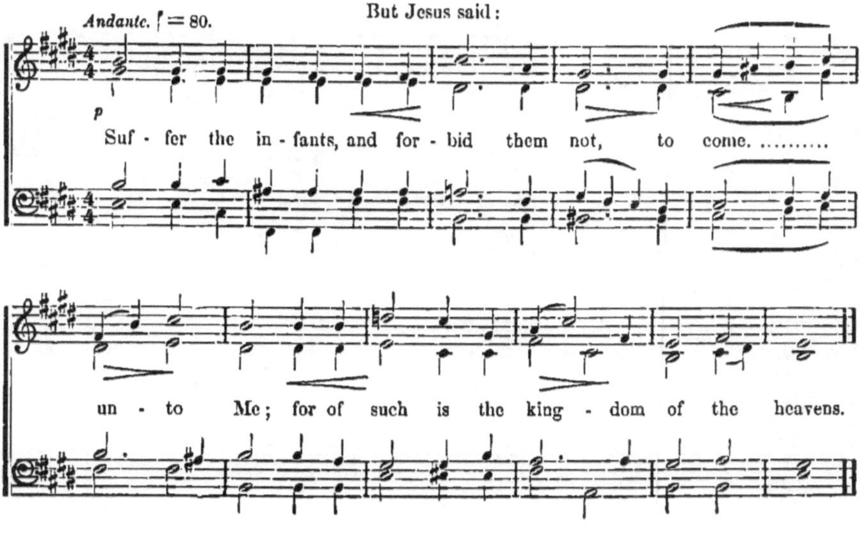
Andante. ♩ = 80.
p
Suf - fer the in - fants, and for - bid them not, to come. ....
un - to Me; for of such is the king - dom of the heavens.

APOCALYPSE XV: 3, 4.

Confession from joy of heart that the Lord alone is the Saviour, the Redeemer, and the God of heaven and earth, who created all things, and who alone is to be loved and worshipped.

And they sang the song of Moses the servant of God, and the song of the Lamb, saying:—

Maestoso ♩ = 63.

Great and won-der-ful are Thy works, O Lord God Al-migh-ty; just and true are Thy ways, O King of saints...... Who shall not fear Thee, O Lord, and glo-ri-fy Thy name? for Thou a-lone art ho-ly; wherefore all .... na-tions shall come and a-dore be-fore Thee, be-cause Thy judg-ments are made man-i-fest.

DEUTERONOMY VI: 4, 5.

The Lord God is to be loved from all that is in man: from the will, where is the good of love, from the understanding, where is the truth of faith, which two are of the internal man, and from those things which are of the will, and of the understanding in the external man.

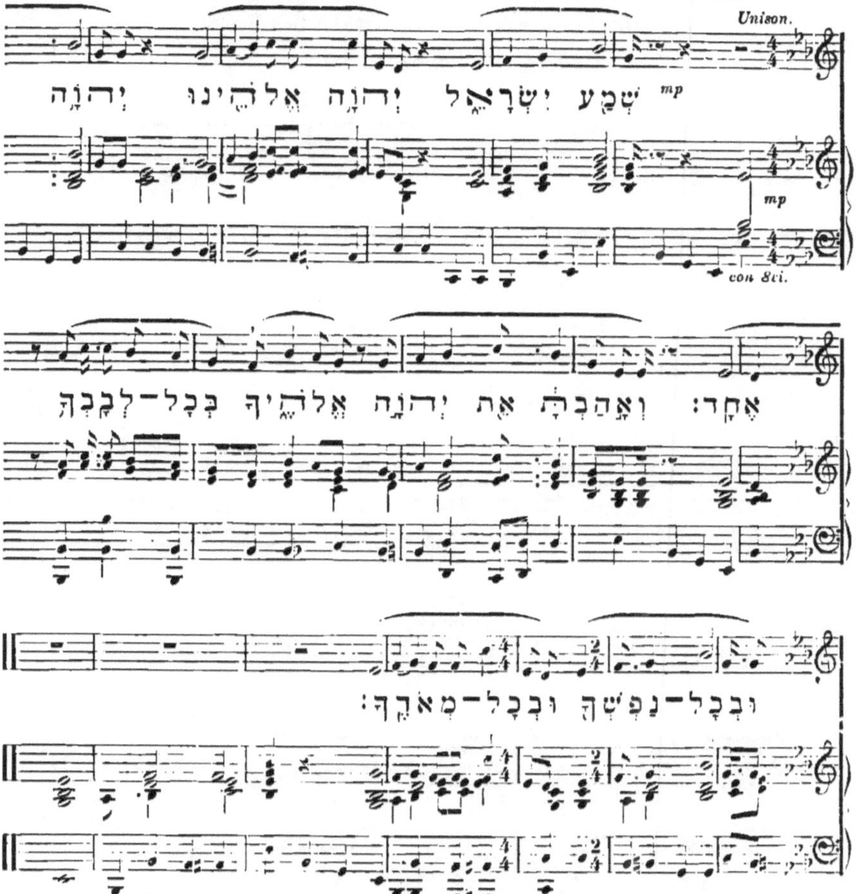
Unison.
mp
שְׁמַע יִשְׂרָאֵל יְהוָה אֱלֹהֵינוּ יְהוָה
mp
con 8vi.
אֶחָד: וְאָהַבְתָּ אֵת יְהוָה אֱלֹהֶיךָ בְּכָל־לְבָבְךָ
וּבְכָל־נַפְשְׁךָ וּבְכָל־מְאֹדֶךָ:

TRANSLATION.—Hear, O Israel, the LORD our God is One LORD. And thou shalt love the LORD thy God, with thy whole heart, and with thy whole soul, and with all thy forces.

LUKE II: 14.

The angels of heaven confess and worship the Lord from joy and gladness, because of the birth of the Saviour of the World.

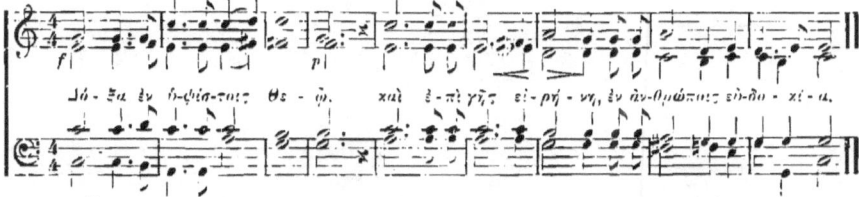

f
p
Δό - ξα ἐν ὑ-ψίσ-τοις Θε - ῷ. καὶ ἐ - πὶ γῆς εἰ - ρή - νη, ἐν ἀν-θρώποις εὐ-δο - κί - α.

TRANSLATION.—Glory in the highests to God, and upon earth peace, in men good pleasure

PSALM CL.

The New Church and at the same time the New Heaven.
Celebration and Worship of the Lord.

הַלְלוּ יָהּ ׀ הַלְלוּ־אֵל בְּקָדְשׁוֹ הַלְלוּהוּ בִּרְקִיעַ עֻזּוֹ: הַלְלוּהוּ
בִגְבוּרֹתָיו הַלְלוּהוּ כְּרֹב גֻּדְלוֹ: הַלְלוּהוּ בְּתֵקַע שׁוֹפָר הַלְלוּהוּ בְּנֵבֶל
וְכִנּוֹר: הַלְלוּהוּ בְּתֹף וּמָחוֹל הַלְלוּהוּ בְּמִנִּים וְעֻגָב: הַלְלוּהוּ בְצִלְצְלֵי־
שָׁמַע הַלְלוּהוּ בְּצִלְצְלֵי תְרוּעָה: כֹּל הַנְּשָׁמָה תְּהַלֵּל יָהּ הַלְלוּיָהּ:

PSALM CL. *Continued.*

He should be worshipped from every affection of good and truth.

PSALM CL. *Concluded.* 387

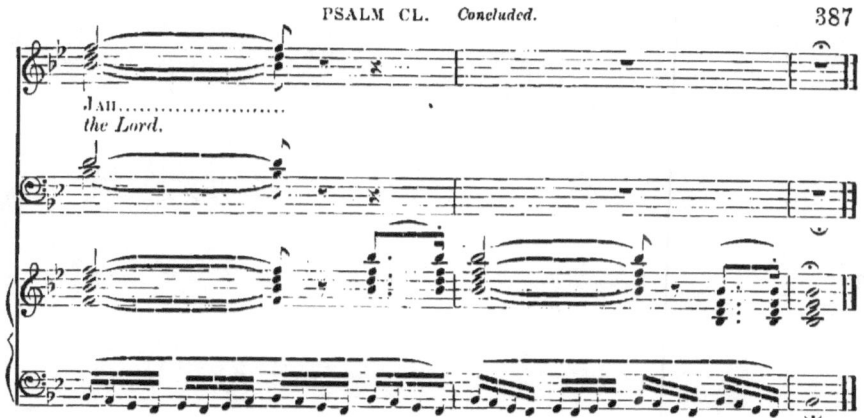

APOCALYPSE IV: 8.

The Lord alone is God, and hence He alone is to be worshipped, who is Infinite and Eternal, and Jehovah.

TRANSLATION.—Holy, Holy, Holy, Lord, the God, the Omnipotent, who was, and who is, and who is to come.

www.ingramcontent.com/pod-product-compliance
Lightning Source LLC
Chambersburg PA
CBHW032020220426
43664CB00006B/313